HOW TO MAKE YOUR POINT
without
POWERPOINT
50 WAYS TO PRESENT EFFECTIVELY

HOW TO MAKE YOUR POINT
without POWERPOINT
50 WAYS TO PRESENT EFFECTIVELY

DOUGLAS KRUGER

PENGUIN BOOKS

Published by Penguin Books
an imprint of Penguin Random House South Africa (Pty) Ltd
Reg. No. 1953/000441/07
The Estuaries No. 4, Oxbow Crescent, Century Avenue, Century City, 7441
PO Box 1144, Cape Town, 8000, South Africa

www.penguinbooks.co.za

First published 2015

1 3 5 7 9 10 8 6 4 2

Publication © Penguin Random House 2016
Text © Douglas Kruger 2016

PUBLISHER: Marlene Fryer
MANAGING EDITOR: Janet Bartlet
EDITOR: Nichy du Plessis
PROOFREADER: Mark Ronan
COVER DESIGNER: Sean Robertson
TEXT DESIGNER: Ryan Africa
TYPESETTER: Monique van den Berg

Set in 11.5 pt on 14.5 pt Adobe Caslon

Printed and bound by DJE Flexible Print Solutions, Cape Town

ISBN 978 1 77022 923 5 (print)
ISBN 978 1 77022 924 2 (ePub)
ISBN 978 1 77022 925 9 (PDF)

To Mom and Dad, for raising me in a household that revered great and memorable storytelling, while remaining utterly and perpetually baffled by numbers and statistics.

CONTENTS

Having the information is only half the job.
Making it *come alive* is the balance.

Think again.

A VERY, VERY SHORT HISTORY
OF PUBLIC SPEAKING

500 million BC to the present

Bubbles in the primordial soup. Things swim, grow bored, then venture onto land. A rock arrives from outer space killing a lot of rather large lizards. Mammals replace them. They babble and chatter to one another, warring and mating. The less hairy ones develop a proud oratory tradition that sets them apart. Empires rise and fall, wars are waged, riots fill the streets and in a faraway land, a president with a snappy tie thumps a lectern and says, 'Yes we can!'

That covers the history of public speaking. Now let's get practical. How do you present without slides?

Putting the world to sleep since 1990

'Death by PowerPoint.' That's the commonly used term, bandied about by bored delegates over black coffee, and sent covertly from phone to phone in stuffy boardrooms. It was coined by Angela R. Garber. 'PowerPoint poisoning' is another such term, and it had its genesis in *Dilbert*, the office-life comic strip by Scott Adams.

PowerPoint is a much maligned program. In the beginning, it was a really good idea. It is not the program's fault that it all went wrong.

Microsoft's proud creation suffers a similar PR problem to money. Universally acknowledged as the root of all evil, money has been falsely accused. What the Good Book actually says is that 'the *love* of money is the root of all evil'. Similarly, it is the obsessive, compulsive, yearning, mindless, brainwashed, mewling, needling, squirming, frightening *need* for PowerPoint that is actually the problem. Not PowerPoint itself.

No, PowerPoint is not inherently evil. Nor, for that matter, are the atomic bomb, poison gas or timeshare salespeople. It is simply how they are inflicted upon society that is evil. And through no fault of its own, PowerPoint has been used to visit more pain on professional people, in a shorter space of time, than global recession and multilevel marketing combined.

The problems are:

- misuse; and
- overuse.

Undereducated presenters will put together shocking little abominations and then present them to the world with a grin: 'Look! Isn't my baby beautiful?!' Misuse generally occurs when we bravely pack the entire script of *War and Peace*, and the history of Western economic develop-ment, onto a single slide, then say things like, 'I know you probably can't *see this, but...*' And, like stories about starfish being tossed back into the sea, overuse has strangled the efficacy out of PowerPoint until, sadly, Bill's brilliant little baby has been rendered a psychological sedative.

More zombies have been created in conferences through PowerPoint poisoning than by any other single cause. At the time of writing this, the number is approximately half the human race – lending credence to the fear that half of us will ultimately rise up and eat the other half. PowerPoint has crossed over to the Dark Side.

As a professional speaker, I vividly recall the conferences at which I've heard a presenter open with, 'I won't be using a single PowerPoint slide in my presentation', only to receive thunderous applause, sometimes from a standing audience. People appreciate the honest connection afforded by a real human being without a canned pitch.

So, how did this curious force rise to power? How did we miss the signs of impending apocalypse?

The rise of the machines

The program was originally developed under the title Presenter, but was renamed PowerPoint before its launch on 22 May 1990. It was bundled together with the Microsoft Office package and has enjoyed that symbiotic relationship ever since.

Companies like Apple have produced alternatives – Keynote in that particular case – but PowerPoint remains the flagship.

By 2012, it had been installed on over a billion computers and claimed 95 per cent of the market share for presentation software. *Wikipedia* estimates that it is used around 350 times per second globally. In other words, blink, and nearly 500 audiences have been exposed to it. As self-propagating systems go, PowerPoint looks at the Ebola virus and sneers, 'Amateur!'

Truly, the machines have taken over.

Sadly, PowerPoint is no longer as effective as it once was in helping us to communicate clearly and effectively. In fact, it tends to hinder communication. Instead of making thoughts come alive, it smothers them in molasses of sameness. It turns brilliance into bullet points and inspired ideas into horrid little charts, graphs, dots, dashes, pies, columns, tables and squiggly lines. It takes the passionate free flow and colourful versatility of language, and reduces it to a sort of boxed-in accompaniment. Because of the way in which its parameters force thought through certain pre-determined channels, it makes us all sound horribly similar.

Think of it like music. The best presenters sound like the score to *The Lord of the Rings*. Presenters stuck to PowerPoint are playing 'Chopsticks' with a metronome: clonky-clonky-clonky-clonk ...

One of its great downfalls is that, no matter how well you use its myriad neat tricks, everyone else is using it too. And so even the most trained and effective PowerPoint devotees are just marginally more developed sheep.

I want to be frank, lest I am ever accused of sneaking up on you with a covert agenda: I don't like PowerPoint. And, as someone who speaks full-time for a living, trains executives and sales teams to speak so that they can sell and lead like champions, competes in speaking contests, and writes books and articles on speaking – I feel I am qualified to make this assertion. And I can prove that my stance is correct, too. Just look at the information on the following slide ...

So what are the advantages of not using it?

I count eight distinct advantages:

1. By not using it, you'll stand out from the crowd

If everybody does it, and you don't − and your presentation is better − they will notice. The key, of course, is that it must actually be better. But that's why you're reading this book. We are not just dumping a tool here. We are going to replace it with superior ones. My goal is not to deprive you of a resource. It is to teach you better speaking techniques.

2. It enhances the level of connection you are able to create with your audience

During your presentation, they will feel the full electrical crackle of human animation, whereas the audiences of PowerPoint diehards will feel only a close approximation of life − a sort of Frankenstein's monster.

This crackling connection will be felt right from the beginning of your presentation, which is the critical time when your audience is evaluating you and secretly wondering whether or not this talk will be worth their while. Most presenters open by showing a bold headline and then reading it out loud − which is amateurish − or, worse, by fiddling with a problematic projector. *You* will simply walk out in front of your audience, command the space, connect with them visually and psychologically, take hold of their minds and imaginations, look every bit the confident thought leader, and begin a powerful mental journey in which you guide them towards your desired outcomes.

The crackling connection will then be felt right through to the end of your presentation, at which point they will be so completely *with you*, that you will experience the highs of agreement and applause. Or, at the very least, the satisfaction of a non-comatose audience.

3. It changes your voice

Ever received that intrusive phone call from a telemarketer, usually around dinnertime? Ever been able to tell beyond all doubt that the person is reading a script at you? You can hear it in the voice. The patterns of speech are not authentic. The same applies when we use rigid Power-Point guidelines: our patterns of speech sound stilted and rehearsed. They become boxed in by the restraints of the format and we rob ourselves of the very fire and conviction that are the heart and soul of public speaking. By trying to cage it, we douse our own magic.

4. It makes you more agile

Dumping PowerPoint gives you agility in your content and agility in your timing.

How often have you sat through a PowerPoint guided tour, thinking that the information being presented just wasn't of any relevance to you? That's because the speaker was stuck to the slides, which they had prepared in advance (or, worse, which the company's corporate guidelines committee had prepared in advance).

A speaker stuck to slides is a terrible thing. The speaker before him may steal his thunder by delivering his message and he will have no choice but to duplicate, because the slides are already done and there's no time to change them.

Worse still is the presenter who knows that the slides are irrelevant: 'I'll just skip past this slide … and this one … and the next one …' Talk about wasting an audience's time! And talk about creating a poor impression of yourself, your brand, your cause or your organisation. It's enough to un-sell a great idea.

When you are not being constrained by slides, you are able to be more agile. You are able to customise your information to *that* audience and to *that* moment. Someone else said what you wanted to say? No problem. Dump that bit. Something interesting happened in the room? Customise your talk to include it. It's as though you have a blank page and, as such, you can be infinitely more creative. Crucially, you will sound like you are speaking directly to your audience, rather than going through the motions.

Also, in terms of agility, you won't be forced to go over time as a result of having too many slides. Because you can edit on the fly, you will be able to chop out whole swathes of irrelevant information, get to the heart of your message and overcome time constraints. People love speakers who keep to time. They buy flowers for them, write songs about them, fling panties at them and immortalise them in marble.

5. It prevents audience switch-off

Most presentations follow the format of a growing explanation, leading to a resolution. In other words, you build your point until the audience finally gets it.

While you are holding your audience in the anticipation phase, they will usually pay attention. But, crucially, as soon as they get it, they will tend to drift off.

PowerPoint slides allow the audience to get it before you have explained it. Presenters will typically build anticipation by beginning to explain their idea, but will then undermine themselves by revealing a slide that resolves the idea before they even speak about it. The audience reads ahead, gets it, and then switches off as they wait for you to catch up.

6. It reduces your stress

Inexperienced presenters tend to assume that not having a PowerPoint guide will make their job more stressful, not less. This is not true. Using PowerPoint effectively constitutes an additional skill set. In other words, PowerPoint represents one more thing for you to be thinking about, when you should be thinking about connecting and persuading.

Also, consider this: if you arrive late for a presentation and have to set up your PowerPoint show, you have added a dimension of stress to the introduction – and a significant one at that. You have complicated the logistics. And it's not uncommon for the equipment to fight back – refusing to cooperate and rendering you PowerPoint-less anyway. If you had intended to use PowerPoint, and then for some reason discovered that you were not able to, you would be worse off than if you had simply prepared not to use it at all.

The PowerPoint-free speaker enjoys a wonderful level of freedom and simplicity. He or she can simply arrive, stroll to the front of the room and begin.

7. You will enjoy your presentations more

Trust me. There is nothing quite like the natural high of being 'in the zone' and having an audience hanging on your every word. PowerPoint slides do not allow you the time and space to get into that zone. They restrict your speaking style to a stop-start, chunk-at-a-time motion. They destroy natural rhythm, which is one part of eloquence.

Yes, they provide a guideline. But they provide the guideline at the cost of oratory form. It's like giving an audience a set, steady drumbeat, because that's easy to remember and follow, rather than giving them Beethoven, which is infinitely more free, infinitely more inspiring.

Give them Beethoven. They'll love you for it.

8. You'll get to see your family at night

Preparing slides can be monstrously, disastrously time-consuming. That's not a big deal for a professional speaker, who might present the finished product hundreds, if not thousands of times in the future, legitimising his or her time investment.

But for Joe Cubicle, who has but one talk to prepare, it can entail hours, even days of preparation. And the preparation is, itself, a false investment in time. Joe is not actively working on persuasive things to say and clever techniques by which to say them. The hours of design work are merely design work – not prep work – because Joe is actually just wasting time tinkering with aesthetics and settings, which are secondary.

A matter of national security?

Because of its lazy ease of use, PowerPoint has not only suffused the corporate world, but has also wheedled its way into education, the military and even space travel. But not everyone lauds or applauds the fact. In fact, some are militantly opposed to it.

Brigadier General Herbert McMaster, of the United States Army, famously banned the use of PowerPoint in briefings. He claimed that they negatively affected the decision-making process by misrepresenting ideas, because the way in which ideas are arranged in slides forces a certain kind of thinking and perception.

It's like I said before: PowerPoint is a metronome. It forces your music into stilted patterns. Apparently, it also does the same to strategic thought.

And Brigadier General McMaster is not alone. In his book, *The Cognitive Style of PowerPoint*, Edward Tufte declares that the program causes 'damaging misrepresentation'. Take the example of how the Boeing Corporation created slides that oversimplified facts presented to NASA officials about possible damage to the space shuttle Columbia during its final launch. They weren't *wrong*: they were just mildly twisted by the internal language structures of PowerPoint. Tufte takes serious issue with 'the language and spirit of this presentation style'.

We tend to think that PowerPoint allows us to be *more* technical and *more* detailed than we might be without it. These authorities assert the exact opposite, saying that free-form language is capable of much greater accuracy than slides with headlines.

There is also a much simpler dynamic at play: the speed at which we get things done in the real world. A man named Jim Nelson, who served as a translator between the American and Russian troops in Bosnia, quotes one of the Russians as saying, 'If we ever had a war, while you are working your PowerPoint, we would be killing you.'

Ouch!

It's just not a get-stuff-done-quickly sort of program. And, sadly, our society has begun to attach disproportionate importance to the very act of *creating* PowerPoint slides, as though this somehow equates to productivity. It does not. Preparing slides is a distraction. It takes time away from the real preparation work, which should be thinking of ways to persuade. If you could persuade in a quicker fashion, then the act of PowerPoint creation is a monumental waste of your time. Tell your boss I said so. And buy him a copy of this book. Because I want a beach house.

But how will I let go of my emotional attachment to PowerPoint? I've been using it for decades now!

Seek therapy. Knock your cranium lightly but repeatedly against a firm surface. Find a trusted medical professional who will use the time-honoured psychological technique espoused by effective master physicians world-wide and tell you to … 'Get over it!'

Actually, it's simple. Ask yourself this question: can you think of a single great speech, from any point in history, or even any point in *your* history, that employed slides? Remember when Winston Churchill rallied the Allies against the might of Nazi Germany by saying, 'As you can clearly see in figure 63 …'? No?

Remember how Obama was elected to power, twice, by his stunning use of charts and graphs? Or how you were persuaded to buy your last car because the salesman's slides were just so beautifully designed?

They don't help us. We just think they do. They are not persuasive. We just wish they were.

Actually, the real problem often does not lie with individuals who present. The real problem faced by the PowerPoint Resistance is convincing dull people in positions of authority that their staff are not slacking off by speaking without slides. Sadly, the sheep mindset is so deeply engrained in corporate – and academic – culture that bosses, professors and conference convenors will look at you askance, with suspicion in their beady little mole-eyes, when you say, 'I won't be using slides.'

'You mean you're not taking this seriously?' they seem to be asking. And your answer is, 'No, I'm taking this seriously enough to listen to the professionals and dispense with a hindrance. I plan to do a good job of this!'

We are actually creating handouts, not slides

Realistically, most PowerPoint slides would function much better as handouts after the fact. I am all for designing excellent handouts, and then using them at the end. We will discuss this as a technique later in this book.

Meanwhile, a note of encouragement to The Resistance – listen carefully, I will say this only once! Be confident and take charge. It's your presentation, not theirs. If they won't budge, hand them a copy of this book. Feel free to blame me. When they get to the part about the beady little mole-eyes, try not to be in the room.

So, no visual aids then?

Incorrecto! Visual aids add a great deal to a presentation. That's why PowerPoint was invented in the first place. Again, it was a good idea. It's just been used to death.

The whole point behind the program was to help audiences to *see* your ideas. I reiterate that we're not going to merely dispense with a useful tool. We're going to employ alternative tools that will help your audiences to see your points even more effectively.

Do you, oh leader of The Resistance, ever use PowerPoint?

Yes. In fact, I do. But not often. I have four or five major keynotes, and I only use PowerPoint for one of them. And I know how to use it sparingly, professionally, and only in the bits where it's useful.

I also use it at the beginning of a full day's training, when I ask my delegates to stand and introduce themselves. To break the ice, I ask them to tell me ten things about themselves: their favourite car, radio show, sports personality, etc. I put the list up on the screen, so that they can remember the ten things they need to tell me. Then the screen goes off and the real training begins.

Rethinking what your job actually is

So far I've discussed the demerits of using PowerPoint. I've also given some advantages of speaking without it. Now I feel it's important to correctly orientate our thinking. What are we actually trying to accomplish when we present? What's the goal, the point, the *purpose*? If we begin by getting our heads right when it comes to public speaking, by clearly understanding our primary objectives, we will be exponentially more effective.

Using PowerPoint is not the goal. Not using PowerPoint is not the goal either. Each of these approaches is merely a means to an end. So, what are our desired ends?

The first and most important principle I teach, whenever I train anyone in presentation skills, is this: it's not about the *facts*. It's about the *message*.

There is a world of difference between fact and message. Most effective presentations focus on message. Most bad ones are bogged down by facts. Your job is to do message. Facts are only useful insofar as they help you to support and deliver your message. Beyond that, they are useless. Chuck them.

Consider Abraham Lincoln's *Gettysburg Address* – one of the most famous speeches of all time. It took a whopping two minutes and forty-five seconds to deliver, which means, by definition, he could not have packed it full of facts. The entire speech is just one strong message. His goal was to honour the fallen dead and, in doing so, strengthen the resolve of his faction to fight on, by positioning their efforts as noble. Here is the speech:

> Four score and seven years ago our fathers brought forth on this continent, a new nation, conceived in Liberty, and dedicated to the proposition that all men are created equal.
>
> Now we are engaged in a great civil war, testing whether that nation, or any nation so conceived and so dedicated, can long endure. We are met on a great battle-field of that war. We have come to dedicate a portion of that field, as a final resting place for those who here gave their lives that that nation might live. It is altogether fitting and proper that we should do this.
>
> But, in a larger sense, we cannot dedicate – we cannot consecrate – we cannot hallow – this ground. The brave men, living and dead, who struggled here, have consecrated it, far above our poor power to add or detract. The world will little note, nor long remember what we say here, but it can never forget what they did here. It is for us the living, rather, to be dedicated here to the unfinished work which they who fought here have thus far so nobly advanced. It is rather for us to be here dedicated to the great task remaining before us – that from these honored dead we take increased devotion to that cause for which they gave the last full measure of devotion – that we here highly resolve that these dead shall not have died in vain – that this nation, under God, shall have a new birth of freedom – and that government of the people, by the people, for the people, shall not perish from the earth.

Not a single fact. No reference to numbers of the fallen – no charts or graphs to show how much progress they had made. In fact, no specifics at all. Just *message*. And it lives on in history because it touched hearts and minds, and led to action. That's what great speeches and presentations do.

Most speakers and presenters make this fundamental mistake: they believe that their job is to take all of the information they have and dump it on the audience. They believe they are teachers or lecturers. That's wrong. And it's why most speeches are terrible.

Your epiphany for the day

Having the information is only half of your job. *Making it come alive* is the balance. It is my earnest belief that this realisation represents the single most important thing any speaker can ever learn about this craft.

So, PowerPoint was designed to help us make our points come alive. But because it's so badly misused, it tends to kill the efficacy of our points. A truly effective presentation hinges on how well you do two things:
1. Understand the actual goal that your presentation must meet.
2. Use high-impact techniques to meet that goal.

We want to add punch and emphasis to what we say, but understand that *what we say* has primacy. That's why PowerPoint can be useful but is not necessary. And, again, due to overuse, it has become a psychological sedative. We use it because we think it will give us added clout, but its overexposure means that it tends to do the opposite. It vacuums clout from the room and replaces it with grey sameness.

About the points in this book

Let's get into the practicalities of revolutionising the speaking world.

You will notice, oh savvy reader, that some of the sections in this book are long, sprawling frolics into the rolling hills and undulating valleys of an idea, running giddy and carefree over many pages. Others are teeny, tiny, malnourished little things, begging for a home and a warm meal. I have not tried to write sections to an even length for the sake of aesthetic balance. That's PowerPoint thinking: that each idea must fit onto a page.

Instead, each idea has received as much weight as I deem it requires or deserves, relative to the value it offers to you. So, some are short, some are long. Ultimately, it's how you use them.

Also, while you can read the sections out of order, and each will make sense in isolation, they do loosely build upon one another, making consecutive reading a better bet. That said, I hope that after a full reading, you will keep this book and just dip into arbitrary sections, as and when you see a need for them in your presenting career.

Not every idea here will necessarily work in your own particular circumstances. But most of them will. Pick the ones that tickle your fancy, float your boat and fry your eggs, then experiment with them (the ideas – not your eggs).

You'll also find that you can blend concepts together. You are by no means limited to choosing just one out of these fifty ideas. You could probably use up to ten of them in conjunction. Just be cautious not to get so caught up in stage work and techniques that you forget where the real power lies: in speaking with conviction and connecting with human minds. Very often, simplicity wins the day.

Parts 1, 2 and 3

You will notice that the first fifteen ideas, grouped under Part 1, are about structure. These are not physical objects that can be used as replacements for slides, but rather speech styles, guidelines and formats you can use, which will replace the very need for PowerPoint. They will help your audience to get your message, and you to remember it, without requiring slides.

In Part 2 we delve into replacements for slides and clever alternatives for representing information with physical objects and staging techniques. Here is another opportunity to mix and match. You might choose a structural replacement for PowerPoint and add a physical prop to the mix. It's up to you, and the only limit is your creativity. That's what's so great about public speaking.

In Part 3, I grudgingly provide some tips for the proper use of Power-Point, while rolling my eyes and sighing audibly. I do this on the grounds that if, by this stage, you still insist on using the programme, you should at least not commit the most basic cardinal sins in the process.

So, are you ready to dance? Ready to dispense with the crutch and taste freedom? Good! Let's do it!

Here, then, are fifty ways to make your point without PowerPoint ...

PART 1

STRUCTURES THAT REPLACE SLIDES

Use any one of the following fifteen structural approaches in place of PowerPoint, or use a number of them together.

1. Learn to speak well.
2. Deliver one strong message only.
3. Deliver three key points only.
4. Use a problem–solution structure.
5. Tell stories.
6. Use PSA (point – story – application).
7. Use metaphors and similes.
8. Use rhyming aphorisms.
9. Use a representative icon.
10. Use an acronym.
11. Pose a question, then answer it.
12. Use a repetitive 'A' vs. 'B' structure.
13. Use a loose outline, then co-create with your audience.
14. Facilitate a discussion.
15. Hint and reveal.

1. Learn to speak well

It was a brisk, overcast morning outside the Marriott hotel in Dallas, Texas. Droplets of icy water hung from the famous herd of bronze cattle and the cowboys eternally chasing them up the city sidewalks. Unusual weather for Texas, but no one in the hotel was complaining because we were all mesmerised.

A few hundred professional speakers from all over the United States, and a handful of bold adventurers from beyond its borders (including myself, the lone delegate from South Africa), had gathered for the 2012 National Speakers Association Winter Conference, which bore the theme 'Monetise Your Message'. It was to be my first international NSA convention.

We were in a room with a professional speaker named Randy Gage, a high-level earner in the speaking world and our presenter for that particular three-hour session. I had chosen his session arbitrarily. He was one of three options available and I happened to tick his box.

Let me ask, when last did you enjoy a three-hour educational session? Does the prospect generally cause a small part of your soul to wither and die?

But, on that day, when Randy was done, there was a collective, 'Ahh!' of disappointment across the room, and a few calls for him to go on into lunchtime. I remember feeling that I got most of the value of my rather expensive plane ticket in that three-hour session alone.

Was it because of Randy's slides? His supporting visuals? A clever graph?

He had none. Randy Gage has that unusual and valuable talent – he is just a brilliant speaker.

He stood at the front of the room, wearing a suit and an open-necked shirt, simply talking to us for a period of three hours, and we were utterly entranced.

Over the course of this book, I will go into great detail about replacements and alternatives for PowerPoint, but it would be remiss of me not to start by saying that the ultimate alternative to PowerPoint is simple: be a great speaker.

Randy did a number of things that great speakers do, all of which contributed to the success of his three-hour presentation. He:

- angled his information for our benefit, so that it didn't sound like a lecture;
- spoke softly and casually, as though having a good conversation with a friend;
- displayed a calm but assured level of self-confidence that showed he was always in charge and never uncertain;

- varied his vocal tones and rhythms greatly, so that he was never monotonous;
- told stories that illustrated his points;
- used humour to keep us engaged;
- spoke hard truths, resisting the urge to soften, pander, use euphemisms or be politically correct; and he
- took us on a journey, so that when he was finished and we had to leave, it felt like waking up from a trance – the sort of effect you get when you put a good book down and look around at your strange and alien reality.

The best alternative to PowerPoint is mastery of the oratory tradition. If you will learn the fundamentals of public speaking and practise the techniques that help you to connect with, persuade and engage your audience, the need for slides will dissolve all by its sneaky little self.

Speaking well means learning a few of the very simple and easy-to-use techniques that make great speakers memorable.

Over the fifteen points that form Part 1 of this book, I will provide attractive structures for the body of your presentation, but a good opening and a strong conclusion will make a big difference to you. To that end, I would like to provide a bevy of options for opening and closing on a strong note. Think of these options as a buffet. Pick and choose the ones that work best for you or offer you the best opportunity to be creative.

Options for a strong opening
- **Ask a question.** 'When last did you travel abroad? I was in Taipei recently and witnessed some fascinating technology ...'
- **Begin with a quote.** 'Stephen King once said, "Monsters are real, and ghosts are real too. They live inside us, and sometimes, they win."'
- **Start with a dramatic statement or provocative line.** 'This organisation will never compete with the best in the industry ... until we learn these three lessons.'
- **Be theatrical.** Stand on a chair; start at the back; act a part; hold a conversation; draw something.
- **Tell a story.** 'This time last year, my car caught fire. I was en route to this conference, when suddenly ...'

- **Conduct an audience opinion survey.** 'By a show of hands, who here believes that France should be conquered and colonised?'
- **Conduct an audience status survey.** 'Who here was still awake at two o'clock last night? Keep your hands up if you were still awake at three.'
- **Show your polish with a delayed address.** Tell a story, then acknowledge your introducer and/or audience only afterwards: 'Ladies and gentlemen, good morning. The story you've just heard is true.'

Options for a strong conclusion

- **Summarise your main points.** 'So, as we've seen – A, B and C.'
- **End with a call for action.** 'So, tomorrow morning, when you wake up, do this …'
- **End with a question.** 'When will you make the change?'
- **Tie it up to the opening by referencing something from the beginning.** 'And so, just as Stephen King said …'
- **Take questions from the audience.**
- **After repeating a theme throughout your presentation, have the audience repeat it back to you.** 'Yes, we can!'
- **Surprise them with humour.**

For added polish, here are a few don'ts:

- **Don't say, 'In conclusion …',** but if you do, don't say it more than once.
- **Don't disappear immediately afterwards.** Stay and make yourself available.
- **Don't apologise if you feel it didn't go well.** Chances are they didn't notice, and you don't want to draw attention to any errors.
- **Don't peter out** with phrases like, 'I think that's about it.'

So, now that you have a number of options for how to start and end well, let's arm you with specific ways of delivering your main message that are strong enough to obviate the need for slides.

2. Deliver one strong message only

This is the simplest way of speaking without PowerPoint. Simplify your message, so that there is no need for a complex series of explanatory visuals.

Let's use the example of a Monday-morning staff meeting. As the leader, you determine that there are five things you need to tell your team:

1. The upstairs restroom has a blocked drain – please use the downstairs one.
2. It was Stacy's birthday last weekend. Congratulations!
3. Friday will be casual jeans day.
4. Please stop taking teabags home, they are for use on-site only and running out of teabags is just massively irritating for everyone.
5. The quality and focus of work this week will determine whether our organisation lands the biggest client in its history. This would radically alter the total wealth of the organisation and put us on the international map as a major player.

One of these items is immensely important. If you guessed 'casual jeans day', there are caring people who would be willing to pray for you.

Point number five is a simple one. But it is also profoundly important. It is sufficiently important that it is worth separating from the others.

Separate an idea?

Think about this symbolically. If you want someone to notice a dot on a page, would you surround it with other dots? Surround it with lines and squiggles? Or would you simply show one, big, bold dot, smack in the middle of an open, white page?

If the dot is important, you make it stand alone. If you make it stand alone, it will seem important.

In a scenario like the Monday-morning staff meeting, point number five is of such importance that you should actually dispense with the other four. They are distractions and they are diluting the importance of the fifth one.

Fear not, Stacy will still get to hear the off-key strains of 'Happy Birthday'. You just need to delegate those four points to someone else. It would play out like this: a young member of staff who is keen to advance his or her career by taking up a position of leadership and speaking publicly, stands up and covers the first four points, on your insistence. He or she then concludes by announcing that the final item on the morning's agenda is of particular importance and hands over to you, the leader, whose message now stands out in isolation. One strong point.

You deliver your one, strong message. You position your bold dot in the centre of a clean, white page.

You do not go into mountains of detail about how the week will play out – that can be done in separate offline meetings with the different departments. You simply, and powerfully, impress upon everybody the sheer size and importance of this week's work. You have your *rah–rah* moment, inspire and enflame them, and then sit back down.

Short, sharp and powerful. Just like the *Gettysburg Address*, which helped to determine the course of an entire nation. And you haven't used PowerPoint because, when you deliver one strong message only, there is simply no need to.

Now let's get creative. What happens if you don't have an underling to deliver the other four points, but you absolutely have to make that one important idea come alive? You can still do it, and you can achieve it through your method of delivery.

Picture it: your staff are gathered around the meeting room – some in chairs, some standing. You begin the meeting standing casually at the front of the room, where you deliver your four mundane points and congratulate Stacy on the grand accomplishment of popping out of her mom thirty years ago. Stacy feels all special.

Then, your body language changes. You sit down facing them. Your tone of voice drops from fun and frivolous to sincere and serious. You deliver your one, strong message.

Using subtle changes in body language, facial expression and tone, you have signified that everything else was procedural waffle (sorry, Stacy), but that the last thing was terribly, terribly important.

One strong idea, even in the midst of other, less important ones, will stand out as a singularity.

3. Deliver three key points only

We *recall* Winston Churchill saying, 'Blood, sweat and tears.' He *actually* said, 'I have nothing to offer my country but blood, sweat, toil and tears.' That's a set of four. Three, however, is the magical number. For some strange reason – which psychiatrists recognise but can't fully explain – human communication is very effective when grouped in threes.

Threes work very well in communication and in multiple applications. It might be three main points, three illustrating stories or three quick examples. Three repetitive sentences, like, 'We shall rise. We shall stand. We shall fight!' Three of anything, really.

Using the Rule of Three is not only elegant, but also simplifies the amount of information you are required to remember.

At the Toastmasters World Championship of Public Speaking, where competitive speakers are given five to seven minutes to prove their oratory prowess, the approaches tend to fall into two camps: speakers who make one strong point, or speakers who make three smaller, related points. That is by no means the hard-and-fast rule, but over the years, I have observed that it's generally the case.

Two ways of using the Rule of Three

Threes are neat, elegant, eloquent, easy to create, easy to remember, and easy for your audience to follow and digest. You can either divide your one strong point into three story examples that make it come alive, or create a presentation that makes three key points.

However you do it, dividing your talk into three makes it easy for the audience to get, and simple for you to remember. When planning your speech, draw it in the form of a mind map, using three bubbles. Nothing difficult to remember about that.

I would even recommend telling your audience up front to anticipate three things: 'I'd like to share three ways to help you position yourself for promotion at work.' This simple sentence provides a clear guideline for them to follow, and because the number is only three, it also removes the anxiety that you would otherwise create with a phrase like, 'Here are my top twenty-seven and a half recommendations …'

4. Use a problem–solution structure

Many perfectly good ideas are unnecessarily shot down in their infancy because they are proposed without sufficient context. Have you ever pitched a brilliant idea at work, only to have it shot down?

Let's see if we can diagnose the problem. The eager young worker comes up with what is, in fact, a spectacular plan. He dashes to the executive offices of his (older, somewhat cynical) superiors, bursts through the door and gushes it out in one great torrential spew – spit 'n spanners flying. They smile politely and toss him an attaboy for trying. They nudge each other, share a look about the amusing enthusiasm of youth, and then proceed with their own inferior plan.

Or a variation on this theme: the shy, middle-aged woman who is generally happy to keep her head down and do what is expected of her suddenly has an epiphany. She doesn't generally contribute ideas but, in her heart of hearts, she knows that this is a good one. She timidly asks whether she might speak to the senior-level decision-makers, and when they indulgently acquiesce, she plays her idea down as silly, '… but there you have it anyway.'

She, too, is shot down.

In both cases, our presenters have made the same mistake. They have attempted to sell their solution without first properly selling the problem.

Selling the problem

What is a speech if not a sales pitch for an idea? We don't stand up and speak just for the sake of filling time. There is always a point. There is always a purpose. When we speak, we are engaged in the vocation of selling ideas.

For that reason, the more techniques we can learn about the art of persuasion, the better.

When you stand to speak, your mindset should not be merely: 'I hope to get through this ordeal okay.' It should be: 'I'm going to present these ideas so compellingly that people will think differently once I'm done.'

And so we use the problem–solution structure to heighten our persuasiveness. It works on the premise that you need to emotionalise (or sell) the problem before you can properly sell your solution.

To sell the problem, you have to provide context. It's Sales 101. Don't tell us how great your vacuum cleaner is. Tell us how embarrassing it is to have a dirty home. Detail the specifics of a homeowner's problems so that they come alive in the mind: 'You vacuum regularly, but run your hand over the carpet and a film of dirt still comes away on your fingertips. It frustrates you that you could work so hard and still get such poor results.'

Advertisers sell the problem, not the product.

Some of the most effective instructional speeches that I have ever seen have used this format and I recommend it to you. Rather than telling the audience how to manage their money, create an emotional picture of how it looks when it all goes wrong. Rather than simply telling us to lead using your principles, paint a picture of the disasters that have befallen others who have not used them. Rather than simply saying, 'Here is an alternative to PowerPoint ...' detail and emotionalise the problems with using it in presentations.

Your goal as a speaker is to sell an idea, and you will do so much more effectively if you begin by getting your audience emotionally invested in the seriousness of the problem.

Contextualise, emotionalise, sell.

In our examples, if the gushing young man, or the self-conscious woman had opened their pitches with a little bit of detail about the pain that their problem causes, had attached a monetary amount to the problem, or had shown how much productivity is lost because of it, they would have stood a greater chance of prevailing.

I use this technique in almost all of my presentations. In *How to Position Yourself as an Expert*, I begin by discussing how one can work incredibly hard and never break even in the course of a lifetime. I then go on to pose expert positioning and raising personal value as one of the solutions to this pain – explaining that the more highly you are perceived in your industry – the greater your fee for fewer hours of work.

The next time you present an idea, don't start with the idea. Start with the pain. Start with the problem. Sell *that* effectively and they will be craving your solution by the time you arrive at it.

Another upside to this technique is that it allows you to strongly engage your audience, right from the outset, because rather than starting with introductory waffle, you get to start by telling a story, which is always a good idea in public speaking. In particular, your story has an emotional angle that is relevant to that particular group: 'Imagine what your life looks like when this goes wrong ...' You will feel the difference this makes in their level of engagement immediately, and a good start makes you feel good about the rest of your presentation.

Naturally, as you become an increasingly skilled and experienced presenter, you will even find ways to tell negative, problem-based stories in humorous and amusing ways. You could tell a story that gets three or four strong laughs, before coming to a profound conclusion, at which point the audience thinks: 'Yes, I recognise myself in that story.' They enjoy the story, feel the pain, empathise with the problem you're describing, and are eager to hear more about solving it.

5. Tell stories

A time-honoured adage for speakers asserts that stories are the medium of human communication.

There is nothing more powerful than a story to communicate an idea. Tell us, and we might understand. But *show* us, and we will never forget. Jesus made use of parables, which are stories with a point, and the lessons they teach have been passed on through the centuries.

Stories help you to look less preachy and less prescriptive, because they make the point without your having to belabour it. The point is intrinsic to the story. Do you feel you spend too much time pointing your finger and telling them what to do? Stories are the answer to this one. They make your point effectively, but diminish the authoritarian, 'because I say so!' impression that we want to avoid.

There are whole books dedicated to the art of using stories in presentations, because they are so profoundly effective. In fact, there are trainers and consultants who make careers out of teaching others how to use storytelling to sell and lead more effectively. But all that we need to understand at this stage is that their use is well worth our while and that they are a wonderful alternative to PowerPoint.

Stories are really the antithesis of PowerPoint. They are its natural opposite, particularly in terms of their effect upon audiences. Where bullet points, lists and graphs invite an audience to switch off (essentially giving the cue: 'Here comes the boring, technical gumpf...'), stories do the exact opposite. They awaken the much-neglected creative side of the mind, giving the cue: 'This bit is real and interesting. This is how it happened to these guys, and it could happen to you.'

By definition, stories require the audience to participate by using their own mental juices. They compel the construction of internal mental imagery, characters, ideas and ideals, according to what you are saying. And the more vivid and interesting your storytelling technique – the greater the total number of neurons you will trigger to fire in their minds. Bullet points can only fire so many neurons.

Stories can incorporate multidimensional drama, tension, colour, mood and emotion, jubilant highs and despairing lows, movement, sound, sight and location, tension and resolution, strategy and outcome. These light up much greater swathes of the audience's minds. This means they'll pay better attention. This means they'll stay awake for longer. This means their total experience of you will be much richer and more satisfying.

What kind of stories?

Here's the good news: you needn't have scaled Everest, wrestled a nest of alligators or spent the weekend with Angelina Jolie to be an effective story-teller. Of course, if you *have* done any of these, they will make great stories and I will personally buy you a beer while you tell me the Angelina one. But it's often the seemingly trivial things that really work well in speech.

In fact, the most useful story material is often culled from the day-to-day stuff of life. A story about how your four-year-old daughter made a hard decision can be used to illustrate the difficulty of wanting something versus making the right choice. A small incident in the office can be used to discuss the entire culture of a corporate company. An incident with a pet hamster running in a wheel can become the basis of an entire motivational keynote. Trust me on this. I've been presenting The Rules of Hamster Thinking for over ten years now.

Storytelling is merely the art of finding an incident that somehow encapsulates, represents or relates to a quality or idea. It can ring with fear as a warning, or tickle with humour.

Stories work their magic on humanity's meaning-seeking minds. Through stories, we get to see, feel, taste, touch and hear what you mean. Instead of delivering dry, intellectual points, suddenly you are delivering whole moods and states of mind. And moods and states of mind are persuasive. And, once again, what is a speech if not a persuasive sales pitch for your idea?

So, how are stories a replacement for PowerPoint slides? Simply put, if you can remember a couple of stories and the points that they make, you can remember your entire speech.

I am a fan of using mind maps to create speeches. However, I do use one slight variation on Tony Buzan's classic spider-diagram, as he described it in *The Mind Map Book*. I prefer to work from the top of a page to the bottom.

Here is a basic, diagrammatic representation of my Hamster Thinking speech:

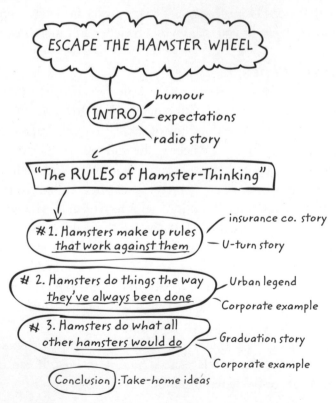

See how easy it would be to remember an entire hour of speaking using this format? There are only three major points. In each case, I tell a series of stories (usually three as well), to make each point come alive.

I need only remember three basic points and the stories that accompany them. Who needs cue cards for that? What's the point in using PowerPoint?

Stories are a speaker's very best friend.

If you have ever interacted with professional speakers, you might be familiar with the concept of signature stories. In essence, a signature story is one that that speaker has become famous for, which, in itself, tells you something about the efficacy of storytelling.

The more regularly you present, the more you will find that certain key stories work better than others. You might find yourself reusing them for different purposes, and I would encourage you to do so. Develop your stock of signature stories. Collect and hoard them like treasure. A signature story can be developed and refined over time so that it becomes more polished and more effectively delivered with every occasion.

And don't think for a second that people resent your reuse of a signature story. You'd be amazed by how often professional speakers are hired on the strength of a story alone. A CEO might say something like: 'Come tell that story for my staff,' rather than, 'Come and give that presentation to my staff.' This is an important distinction that shows just which part of the presentation people respond to.

6. Use PSA (point – story – application)

PSA is easy to remember and it is one of the most effective structures around. It's a comprehensive variation on the 'tell stories' approach, and will work in almost any presenting scenario. I highly recommend it. And I use it often. You make your point, tell an accompanying story, then explain to the audience how they can use your thought, idea or proposal in their world. In other words, after making the point and telling the story, you show them very clearly what to do about it.

You can also shake it up by changing the order. Open with the story that leads up to the point, then provide the application. When you start with a story, you hook people's interest up front. The fact that they don't yet know what the point is will keep them with you by creating mystery and suspense. They will also feel a certain sense of satisfaction when they arrive at the *aha!* moment. That's good theatre!

The real skill in this approach lies in how clear and relevant you can make the application. Once you've made your point and told your story (or vice versa), don't cop out with a vague application, such as, 'So, go out there and live your dream!'

The more specific you can be – the more clarity you can provide the audience on what they should do about it – the more they will appreciate it. All presentations should be audience-centred anyway. Application is the point at which you connect all the dots for them and show them how your point, argument or proposal can become a reality in their lives. It's the call to action, the to-do list, the instruction manual that they take home and use. It's the practical, easy-to-implement answer to their lingering question: 'So what?'

Tip

Audiences increasingly want very specific how-to messages, rather than just pie-in-the-sky concepts. In my keynote speech How to Position Yourself as an Expert, I go to great lengths to give very practical to-do items for my audience. I'm often thanked afterwards for giving a message that was useful, rather than vague. And for not only pointing them down the right path, but also for giving them a distinct shove, so that they know precisely how to start walking.

Practical how-to is highly appreciated.

Now go ye and do likewise! And PSA will be your guide.

7. Use metaphors and similes

I love the kind of comparisons that can be made using similes and metaphors. Metaphors are my thing. I teach the power of metaphors when I train expert positioning (in a section on how to communicate with high impact). I teach it in public-speaking courses, and I bore my friends and family with it around coffee tables. When no one's watching, I sneak onto illicit metaphor websites. One day I'll admit that I have a problem.

Similes and metaphors provide a powerful core structure and are used widely by professional speakers. They have all the advantages of stories, plus a few more, which is why I've devoted a significant percentage of this book to using metaphors in presentations.

As a simple example of how a metaphor might be used, I have a presentation called Big Bum Thinking. (Author pauses to imagine the reader doing a double take.) I open by asking, 'Do you blame the jeans, or do you hold yourself accountable for the size of the bum?' I then extend this humorous and surprising metaphor into a fairly serious presentation on the mindset of victimhood. This single core structure, captured and expressed in a simple metaphor, drives the entire hour-long keynote.

It doesn't just drive the keynote: it makes it memorable. It provides an easy little verbal capsule by which people can reproduce it for others: 'He spoke about whether you blame the jeans or own the bum.' Neat and snappy. It's much more clunky to explain, 'He spoke about how we allow ourselves to think like victims and how we should be more proactive.' A metaphor neatly sums up the gist of the thing in a pithy way.

Metaphors are every bit as powerful as stories, but with the additional advantage that your metaphor doesn't actually have to be true. The jeans metaphor doesn't rely on a specific story that actually happened. It relies merely on a representative idea: the notion of blaming something outside of yourself. For that reason, you can make up any metaphor to fit any point that you're trying to make.

The comparative power of similes and metaphors lets you employ the power of imagination. You get to access and draw from the endless universe of: 'It's like ...'

Some major advantages of metaphors
- They help you to sum up complex ideas quickly.
- They are imaginative and stimulating to the human mind.
- They are memorable because they are quirky.
- They are talked about outside of your presentation, because people remember them. You have effectively armed them with a cool thing to say to advertise ... you. This makes your ideas go (as speaker Brian Walter puts it) verbally viral.
- They save great bucket-loads of time.

- They allow you to bring creativity and juiciness to even the most boring, technical explanations.
- They allow you to use storytelling techniques with all the advantages thereof – even when you don't have a corresponding real-life story.

Metaphors can be used to liven up absolutely anything. Here's a quick example, applied to the subject of speaking itself: they may be rare, but some presentations are like watching Sofía Vergara go by in a short skirt. They compel your attention. And if the presenter really knows his stuff, Sofía might even stop, indulge a wink and blow a kiss your way. But, sadly, most are not. Most presentations are more like a Sunday afternoon in a dilapidated municipal graveyard ... in bad weather ... in uncomfortable underwear – while a small dog bites at your foot.

So, if you're determined to treat your next audience to Sofía, where do you start? Turning your presentation from dust and bones into Sofía is actually not difficult. Your task is to take the most important and poignant facts and make them come to life. Remember, the facts are not the important thing. A speech is not an information dump. The *impact* that the facts make – the *message* that they communicate – that's what truly matters.

And stories and metaphors are the two legs that Sofía stands on. Use them well, and they will give you impact. Use them well, and you will never need another slide.

Creating Sofía from scratch

Using stories, similes and metaphors is easy. It is simply the act of saying, 'It's like ...', and then creating a small series of mental pictures that capture the heart and soul of the thing.

For example, an American professional speaker describing what it's like to speak for the youth market says, 'You have to smuggle your messages in in-between stories. You have to be like a motivational ninja!'

This particular metaphor has had the added advantage of creating humour.

Stop! You're killing us!

In 2010, I received a call from a lady who headed up the marketing division for a financial-services company. She had an interesting problem. The previous year, she had asked her chief financial officer to present a nationwide roadshow and speak face-to-face with the investors and customer base.

This was a great idea – specifically because of the powerful connection that public speaking can create. The trouble was, he turned out to be an incredibly boring speaker.

The year 2010 rolled around and she asked him to do it again. But this time, he was asked to present to his own staff first as a practice run (and – covertly – as a boredom barometer).

After the presentation, consensus among the staff was that it would constitute cruel and unusual punishment to subject actual human beings to such a presentation. Furthermore, to do it to paying customers was not only inadvisable, but quite possibly in violation of the Geneva Convention.

That's when I got the call.

'Please make this presentation interesting!' was the brief.

So I sat with the chief financial officer. He showed me the collection of sixty-four separate slides, with charts and graphs and squiggly lines, indicating in excruciating detail, the intricacies of how the market had behaved over the course of the past year. Now, I'll admit that financial reports have never particularly interested me. But I'm willing to go out on a limb and suggest that even the most diehard number cruncher would have found this mildly paralysing.

I asked him a simple question: 'What are you trying to tell them here? Boiled right down to its absolute bare basics, what's the message that all of this is telling?'

A good-natured man, he smiled, scratched his head, frowned a little, then said, 'I guess what I'm trying to say is that this time last year, we were headed into recession, and they were terrified. We were quite scared too. But we made a lot of good decisions for them, and now we seem to be coming out of the worst of it. Things are picking up again.'

Sixty-four slides to say *that*?

That was his message. That's what he was actually trying to tell them.

The slides were merely proof, but why did he need proof? These people already bought into him and believed the things he said. Proof was largely unnecessary. Just tell them what they need to know.

So, we dispensed with the slides and after a little haggling, we replaced them all with a single metaphor.

When he finally stood before his clients on the all-important roadshow, the Chief Financial Officer said: 'This time last year, we all wandered into a darkened forest, and you were afraid. You turned to me for guidance. What you didn't know was that I was equally scared. But that wasn't good enough. We knew you needed solid leadership, and so we dug deep. We pulled on over a hundred years of our collective experience, and sought real answers. We found a glimmer of light in one direction ... took you by the hand and led you that way. We are proud to say that we are now emerging from the forest, and the choices we made for you were the right ones!'

He then made all of his slides, with their detailed charts and graphs, available to the audience as handouts afterwards. If they really wanted to crunch the numbers and get into the nitty-gritty, they could do so. But the message was more important than the facts that informed it, and we used a metaphor to make that message come alive.

If you used to watch *Top Gear*, you might have heard the skill with which Jeremy Clarkson made dry car facts sizzle with sexiness. Clarkson was the undisputed master of the modern metaphor. His genius lay in taking masses of technical information and condensing it into simple – get it in one go – sound bites. Here are a few of his gems:

- 'It was a bit like putting a sticking plaster on a leaking nuclear missile!'
- 'Look at the way it's shaped. It looks like a dog hunkering down to do its business.'
- 'Most supercars make you feel like you're wrestling an elephant up the back stairs of an apartment building. But this one is like rubbing honey into Keira Knightley!'
- 'This thing has so much torque, it could tear a hole in time!'
- 'It's about as feminine as a burst sausage!'

And from Jeremy's co-presenter Richard Hammond:
- 'It doesn't even look like a saloon. It looks like a DB9 that's taken Viagra.'
- 'Giving the Porsche a rear-mounted engine is a bit like building a pyramid with the pointy bit at the bottom.'

The next time you're toiling away at a PowerPoint presentation, ask yourself whether you are creating impact, or simply listing facts. If you find you've done nothing but record dry details over sixteen slides, consider whether you can do better. You may want to try your hand at turning fact into impact. Your tools are simple: stories and metaphors.

Appeal to the imagination and you will be memorable. You will have impact. Your presentation will be the intellectual equivalent of Sofía Vergara catching your eye and blowing a kiss!

Certainly, you can show a busy graph depicting the ins and outs of any idea. Or you could simply use a metaphor that captures the essence of the idea, and say, 'It's like …'

Metaphors sum up complex ideas quickly. Most of the detail in corporate presentations is superfluous because there is a world of difference between mere information and actual message. Information requires graphs; messages can be made with metaphors.

Professional speakers and trained toastmasters rarely use fussy Power-Point graphs. They know that having information is only half of a speaker's job. Communicating that information in memorable and impactful ways is the full obligation.

Using metaphors for persuasion

I once worked with a group that was pitching to a large bank. It was a deal worth retirement money, which meant that there was no leeway for sloppy presenting. These are the design philosophies we followed while workshopping the presentation:
- The client knows who you are, so strip your slides of company history.
- Charts and graphs are psychological sedatives – find better, more impactful ways to convey information.
- Self-referential headlines are unnecessary. Why head a slide with

'Presentation to Bank on 1 October', when people from that bank are sitting watching that very presentation on that very date? Do they really need to be told what's happening in front of them? The greater the clutter, the less the impact.

- The client is nervous about the problem that they need solved. And that's why you're pitching to them. You are one of many competitors bidding for the work – all of whom have similar product offerings. Therefore, your understanding of the seriousness of their problem and your ability to convey that understanding is more important than your product specifics. Yes, you can list a litany of facts about your product. But that won't necessarily land the deal. The important message is:
  - ○ We truly grasp the complexity and seriousness of your problem.
  - ○ We appreciate the consequences that you face if your problem remains unresolved.
  - ○ We are emotionally invested in completely solving it for you and have the expertise to do so.
  - ○ We will lead you through the entire process and make it easy. Then you can tag on a sort of: P.S. This is the product that we'll use to do it.

So, part one of your preparation should be designing your presentation message to meet the goal. Part two is more creative. This is where you decide how to make an impact. In other words, how do you make those points truly come alive?

Using a metaphor as a theme

I am a great advocate of the themed presentation. For the Great Bank Pitch of 2011, I designed a simple theme that the presenters could continually refer to throughout their pitch. We called it 'Feet in the Fire'. The bank was facing a problem related to impending compliance legislation. They knew they would be in significant trouble if they didn't become compliant. My client's product would help them to do so.

But rather than harp on about the product, we emotionalised the problem:

'You are already standing with your feet in the fire. Let your competitors get burnt through inaction; we plan to pull you from the fire. We're not just here to sell you a product. We want to completely solve your problem. Here's how …'

This simple metaphor shows a deeper understanding of what the bank was actually trying to solve, and the consequences if they failed to do so. It also reignites buyer fear, which was the basis of their compulsion to seek out a solution in the first place.

What this technique does not do is go into excruciating technical detail about how the product works. Sure, we include enough to show credibility, but remember that high-level buyers will not actually be operating the product themselves. So, it is strategically clever to let your competitors do the mind-numbing product demos (going into great and irrelevant technical detail) while you cut through the clutter with a strong message instead.

Themes are powerful when it comes to making your message come alive. The simpler and more visual they are, the better. These are some of the themes I have developed for past clients:

- Emerging from the Forest (for the chief financial officer, after the recession).
- Hands Pressed Against the Glass (an appeal to help those who are poor but desperately trying to break into an industry).
- The Dominoes are Aligned (for a CEO whose strategy was in place, and now needed the cooperation of a number of branches to carry out his vision).
- Dyeing the Water vs. Stirring the Undercurrents (for a training company who wanted to show that they don't just achieve surface-level results – they go deeper and change behaviour).
- The Pie-Man and the Guru (for my keynote on why it's more lucrative to position yourself as an industry expert, than to be seen as a low-level cold-caller).

So, when pitching for The Big One, remember that it's not about credentials. It's about expressing your understanding of their problem and showing that you truly get their scenario and their pain. Then explaining how you plan to solve it for them, using vivid mental imagery. That's all. And that's enough.

8. Use rhyming aphorisms

Turn of phrase always pays. Save them time and make it rhyme.

I am an advocate of the idea that clever language is much more memorable than a clever slide. Metaphors and similes are probably my favourite figures of speech, but devices such as rhyme can be powerful too. And there's science behind the idea.

In his international bestselling book, *Thinking, Fast and Slow*, Nobel Prize winner Daniel Kahneman has a great deal to say about how simple but memorable language can help us to be both persuasive and memorable.

He shows that a short, memorable aphorism – and particularly one that rhymes – will be judged as more insightful and more memorable than longer phrases, or ones that do not rhyme. He cites an experiment in which participants read phrases like:

- woes unite foes;
- little strokes will tumble great oaks; and
- a fault confessed is half redressed.

Other participants in the experiment were then asked to read the same sentiments, expressed in aphorisms that did not rhyme:

- woes unite enemies;
- little strokes will tumble great trees; and
- a fault admitted is half redressed.

The aphorisms are believed to be truer and more insightful when they rhyme. They are also more memorable. But, a word of warning: in the same breath, Kahneman says that using overly complex language (as students might do when trying to impress professors) has the exact opposite effect of a rhyming aphorism. In fact, it consistently depicts poor intelligence and creates impressions of low credibility.

Simple, powerful lines, and rhyming lines in particular, can form an excellent framework for a presentation. Use a single such line to make your one major point, or use three such lines to structure a complex set of ideas. In each case, deliver that line powerfully. It is the central tenet of what you are saying and it should express and encapsulate the entire idea that you would like them to take home.

Interestingly, Kahneman also has a great deal to say about how the human mind is simply not evolved to think in terms of numbers and statistics. It is instead finely attuned to pictures, stories, patterns and small-scale illustrations that represent a larger idea. He has spent a lifetime proving the notion that we don't think in stats: we think in meaningful stories.

So, how would you use rhyming aphorisms as a speech structure? Think of your presentation in terms of waves, which have peaks and troughs. Your climax – the crest of the wave – is the power line: the rhyming aphorism. You would build an argument for your point, using either logical arguments or storytelling (or both), until you have built up to your line. You deliver the line: the climax – the crest of the wave. And then you drop back down again. If you have more than one rhyming aphorism, that would represent your next wave. Start building once again.

These crests and falls build a wonderful natural rhythm into your speaking, and I would encourage you to be just a little theatrical in their use. Subtly build in speed, volume and intensity en route to your power line. Once you get there, deliver the line as though it is the wisdom of Moses! Then let the energy drain from your voice, so that you're back down to a natural, chatting tone. Begin to build again.

Do this naturally enough, and the audience won't even notice it happening. They will simply become caught up in the growing intensity of your point. Then relax a little after each release.

9. Use a representative icon

Icons are similar to similes. Both are abstract forms of representation. The difference between them, though, is that rather than using imaginary 'what if?' constructions, icons are descriptions of real things that can stand for something.

Generally, an icon will be a simple thing that represents a bigger idea by extrapolation. For instance, an economist who wants people to understand the idea of inflation might pick on an obvious icon, such as a Big Mac burger. He or she would then speak about the rising cost of a Big Mac over time (one small item that represents the bigger picture).

The economist's goal might be to point out that people underestimate how much they need to save for retirement. To make that idea come alive, he or she might show how much a Big Mac cost in 1990, how much it costs today, and how much it may cost in twenty years.

This form of illustration can have significant shock value. By using a simple, iconic object that everyone can relate to, you help the audience to get the bigger picture. It simplifies the complex and makes it accessible. It takes a large, abstract idea and makes it specific. This kind of extrapolation is typically best achieved by using the small to represent the large, or the simple to represent the complex.*

Let's say that you're discussing the poor corporate culture in a company. It's one thing to say, 'The culture is bad', which is broad and vague. It's another and more vivid thing entirely to tell a horror story about one iconic representation (for instance, an ineffective employee and a horrifying incident of gross incompetence), and then extrapolate.

This is how you might use such an illustration: 'I'd like you to meet Johnny. Johnny is twenty-three, and he works here because he has to – not because he wants to. Johnny is supposed to be helping the sales team in his role as technical support. But Johnny has an interesting view on his role. He sees successfully landing new business as nothing more than winning more work. So he does his level best to sabotage the sales team. He gets paid the same either way, and so, he'd much rather work less.

Now imagine if you have thirty Johnnys working in this company. Some are in sales, some are in tech support and others are in management. Each of them is subtly sabotaging their bit of the machine. Imagine how quickly, and how completely, this company will implode.'

This way, instead of a vague notion like bad corporate culture, you have some specific representative imagery about how things can go wrong.

If you're feeling intellectually astute, you may have noticed that this last example made use of both icon and metaphor. Yes, I'm that awesome!

Most of my speeches are entrepreneurial in nature – teaching and encouraging audiences to be enterprising. In some of my professional keynote speeches, I use the icon of a box of baby formula. I tell a story about

---

* (For a stirring, emotive example of candles used to represent human lives in the face of annual murder rates in South Africa, read this article by author and speaker, Clem Sunter: http://www.news24.com/Columnists/ClemSunter/15-000-lives-snuffed-out-20120926).

overcoming the poverty my family faced when I was young, and how much of an emotional and psychological impact our situation had on me.

Again, it's one thing to tell an audience, 'We were poor.' It's quite another to describe the food baskets that our local church would drop off, and how much it used to burn when I saw the small box of baby formula they had brought for my infant sister. I speak about the mixture of emotions I used to feel: gratitude that someone was helping us out – shame that they had to. I tell my audiences, 'I remember looking at that little box of baby formula and feeling utterly vulnerable. And I remember thinking: "This is not how I want to live."'

In this case, the box of baby formula is an iconic representation of the larger problem of poverty. It's a tiny, specific pin on which to hang a broad concept. It's so specific and emotive that it makes the idea come alive in ways that merely talking about poverty never could.

Building on that idea, icons are useful when you want to talk about a big, vague concept like prosperity or health or synergy – or any other notion that we want them to imagine. Don't just tell them about it – show them what it would look like. Don't just say, 'Imagine yourself as wealthy.' Say, 'Imagine opening your garage door and finding the car of your dreams. And it's yours to drive. And when another dream car comes along, you simply replace the old one with the new one, because you want to. And you can.' Using a car as an icon for wealth makes the concept more real, more specific.

Now test yourself. How would you do that with a concept like health? Or synergy? Or any abstract idea that you often speak about?

Once again, be as specific as you can. Be as evocative and as visual as you can. Try to think of icons that lend themselves to emotive storytelling. One small, specific thing that represents the bigger picture.

10. Use an acronym

'All right, team. To carry out this project, we'll be using the SMART approach. SMART stands for: Systems, Measurement, Application, Results, Tweaking. Let's start by talking about Systems.'

Using an acronym is this manner makes it easy for you to remember your points, plus it's a pithy way to communicate.

Be sure to use a simple, catchy word. Also, be sure to use one that actually relates to what you are speaking about. For instance, if your presentation is titled Process Excellence, think twice about using an acronym like TOILET. Not good! Instead, you may want to go for something like SHINE.

A word of warning about acronyms: they generally look slick and polished in a corporate environment where most presenters don't bother to create anything as artistic as an acronym. But in the world of professional speaking, which is a little more sophisticated, they are sometimes considered a tad cheesy and a smidge overused. Top speakers might use them on occasion, but they will rarely structure an entire talk around an acronym.

Perhaps we should view the acronym the same way that we view sugar: it's sweet, but don't overdo it.

Happily, if you forget where you are in the acronym while delivering your speech, you can simply ask the audience, who will generally volunteer which letter you had reached. But if your fear of forgetting your own acronym borders on the psychotic, and you are lying awake at night imagining elusive letters in trench coats stalking you down dark alleyways, then you can add a simple prop to this technique. You certainly don't need an entire PowerPoint slide to show the letters of your acronym, but you could use a flip chart, or a small flip pad that stands on a table. To be honest, though, it's really not necessary. Rather have faith in yourself, have faith in your acronym, and speak without the hindrance of props.

An acronym is easy to keep track of as you speak, provided you don't go with something complicated, like SUPERFICIALITY. Just stick to STAR. Short, sharp, punchy and to the point. A good acronym can help you to structure and remember your presentation.

11. Pose a question, then answer it

Questions are uniquely powerful – often more so than statements. That's because they require something of an audience. They pick at the mind. They stroke the imagination. They invite the audience to think: to weigh up and consider, to speculate and wonder what the answer might be.

Asking and answering questions effectively create moments of tension and release.

In speaking and presenting generally, I recommend using questions regularly (even rhetorical ones). It is a great way of keeping your audience engaged and it creates the impression that you are in the moment – having a real conversation with your audience – rather than giving them a lecture. Use questions liberally, particularly towards the three-quarter mark, where you are in danger of slipping into 'eyes-switched-off' lecture mode.

Using this structure effectively is a simple case of asking an important question, then answering, then asking the next one and then answering that. And the approach works like this: you pose an important question, leave it hanging in the air for a moment or two, then answer it. For instance, 'What is the single most important lesson a salesperson can ever learn?' (Pause.) 'The answer is ... positioning!'

By delivering information in the form of a question, you build a state of drama and tension. It's more engaging than blandly stating, 'The most important lesson a salesperson can ever learn is positioning.'

From your perspective, the questions serve a different purpose: they are your headlines, your guidelines ... your road map. The questions them-selves form the structure of your speech. If you know your questions, you know the outline of your entire speech.

If you still don't feel entirely confident, take a small, single page with you into the room. DO NOT take a script of your entire presentation. Just have your questions on the page. In fact, don't have the whole ques-tion – just a part of it. For instance, rather than write out: 'What steps could we take to radically improve the health of our local herd of hippos?' write: 'What steps to improve hippo health?' Or better still: 'Steps for hippo health.'

Refer to your notes discreetly. Don't read your question from your notes. Just glance at it, gather your thoughts and turn back to your audience. Connect with them visually, and then ask them, 'So, what steps could we take to radically improve the health of our local herd of hippos?'

Preferably, of course, learn your questions and dispense with any form of notes entirely. You can remember four or five pertinent questions. I believe in you. I've seen your work. You slugger, you!

If this format seems to vaguely ring a bell for you, it might be that you've seen academic textbooks laid out in this fashion. It's quite common for academic writers to open a chapter or section, with a headline that asks a question, and to then answer it in the paragraph that follows.

It may be useful for you to think of your speech according to the visual rhythm of a textbook: **ask**... answer; **ask**... answer; **ask**... answer. The bold headline asks the question, then there is some white space (a pause), and then the question is answered in prose (or a spoken explanation, in your case).

A great advantage of this technique is the way in which it naturally lends itself to an audience-centred delivery. A dusty professor whose job is to disseminate prescribed course information might never bother to customise his message to the audience's needs. He might simply regurgitate everything he knows.

But change your approach to a question-and-answer style, and it will force you to think with an audience orientation. Questions simply work that way. You will be forced to ask yourself, 'What do they want to know?' and as a consequence, you might end up asking questions like:

- 'So, how do you apply this principle in your life?'; or
- 'What difficulties will you face as you experiment with this approach?'; or
- 'So, having done that, what should you do next?'

See how these questions all engage the audience with an 'audience-benefit' approach? Top speakers and presenters use this little oratory trick liberally, sprinkling audience-centred questions throughout their presentations.

Naturally, although I am proposing this as a format to use for structuring your entire presentation, this needn't be its only application. In any style of presentation, using questions that engage the audience will be a good idea. Say, for instance, you decide to use the point–story–application approach. While making your point, you can ask engaging questions. While telling your stories, you can do the same by simply posing a rhetorical question like, 'Have you ever found yourself in this scenario?'

Don't be surprised if your audience uses the opportunity to engage with you when you ask your question. It could be something as simple as a nod of agreement, or (and this happens quite a lot) a raised hand volunteering a full-scale example.

It happens very naturally because questions genuinely do engage the audience. The more you ask questions, the more the audience perceives that this feels like a very real, very natural conversation. They might be tempted to answer without even thinking about it.

This is a good thing. Certainly, you don't want to let it get out of hand, because you might have time constraints, and also because you should retain control over your message and not get sidetracked. But, ultimately, audience involvement is exponentially better than audience disengagement. Manage it well and count it as a blessing. When it happens, you're doing something right.

Questions engage. They make the presentation feel real, vital, lively and spontaneous. They can be used in conjunction with any other delivery technique, or they can actually *be* the delivery technique.

12. Use a repetitive 'A' vs. 'B' structure

This is another highly effective technique, and one that I try to use whenever I can. It has a wonderful theatricality to it and it's simple to do. Essentially, using a repetitive 'A' vs. 'B' structure goes like this: 'Amateurs do *this*, but experts do *that*; amateurs do *this*, but experts do *that*', and so on and so on, as you juxtapose your two opposing ideas.

The back-and-forth rhythm between two opposing qualities or ideas is intellectually attractive and it helps to draw a very clear line between how to and how not to; desirable and undesirable; before and after. Any presentation in which you hope to change audience behaviours from an undesirable to a desirable will benefit from this structure.

It works particularly well with, 'This is how we used to do it. This is how we are now going to do it.' Most leaders will simply speak about 'how we're going to do things going forward', without contrasting it against 'how we used to do things'. The contrast brings clarity to the idea.

'A' vs. 'B' is also compatible with other structures. For example, you could open with a section that uses 'A' vs. 'B' and then transition into something else. You might even end with it.

The comparative 'A' vs. 'B' structure can be used to great comical effect as well. Mark Gungor – one of the world's leading speakers on marriage, and creator of the Laugh Your Way to a Better Marriage seminars – has a very clever (and very funny) presentation, titled Men's Brain, Women's Brain. The title itself uses 'A' vs. 'B'. Essentially, he talks about the differences between men and women in their thinking and approaches to various scenarios. Very simply, he switches back and forth between, 'Men think this way, and women think that way.'

The very rhythm becomes so intoxicating that when he switches from one to the other, the transition alone elicits a laugh. It is a singularly brilliant bit of humorous speaking and I would strongly encourage you to study it. If you'd like to watch the YouTube clip of this presentation, go to: http://www.youtube.com/watch?v=0BxckAMaTDc.

But 'A' vs. 'B' can be used to make the most serious of points as well. There is no rule governing its application. At its heart and soul, its great defining merit is its capacity to clarify by contrast. If you really want to make an idea come alive, present it in opposition to the alternative. The more vividly you present the two, the stronger the distinction becomes. This can be very persuasive.

'A' vs. 'B': contrast and compare. This structure makes your job quite easy when you first sit down to write or prepare your content. It gives you such a narrow, focused guideline that it actually makes writing the speech a relatively simple matter. Sometimes the words simply fall into place once you've decided to go this route.

It is also an easy-to-remember structure, in that all you need to do is recall the key differences you wish to highlight. Let's say you identify five key differences and then form the entire structure of your presentation based on those. Remember the five key differences and you can remember your entire presentation.

I would strongly advise that you rehearse your delivery for this structure, though. You want the 'back and forth' rhythm to be smooth and effortless, rather than clunky and contrived as you struggle to form your thoughts on the fly. Rehearse it a number of times in private before delivering it live to any audience. Get the transitions smooth. Get a handle on how you build your case and which points go in which order. Done well, the 'A' vs. 'B' approach is extremely strong. The framework is memorable and it can be very entertaining.

13. Use a loose outline, then co-create with your audience

This technique is magnificently agile, entrancingly free-form and utterly terrifying!

Intrigued? Then I'll go on. Here's how it works...

As a dyed-in-the-wool, world-class expert on your particular subject, you step out before the audience and tell them what you *can* cover. Then you ask them what they'd like to hear about. Go!

Yes. It's that anarchic. It's loose, it's free, it's fun and it represents the ultimate in impromptu, seat-of-your-pants speaking.

This is very obviously a PowerPoint-free style of presenting, because you cannot anticipate what they will want to hear. And no two such presentations will ever be alike, no matter how many times you speak on the same topic. Although, you will of course have your stock stories and major key points, which will tend to come up repeatedly.

There is an art to doing this well.

You don't want to be so clunky as to start by saying, 'What do you want to know?' That will simply look like you haven't put in any effort. Also – go about it that way and the audience may not volunteer questions. This is because you haven't sufficiently whetted their appetite. You haven't sufficiently proven that you know your stuff backwards, forwards and diagonally. Nor have you seeded their thoughts with leading suggestions for questions to ask. If they don't ask any questions, you have a very silent, very awkward disaster on your hands.

The art lies in piquing audience interest up front, then throwing out strategic hooks to guide them towards the kind of content that you can cover, and getting them sufficiently interested that they want to know more.

On its surface, this may sound unprofessional. However, when it's done well, it looks magnificent. It can actually look better than a prepared presentation.

I remember being downright rapt watching Mark Brown (the Toast-masters International 1995 World Champion of Public Speaking) use this technique. Mark is a big man with an enormous smile and an even bigger personality. His personality is a force of nature.

At a Toastmasters conference where Mark was the guest speaker, he walked out onto the stage and told a couple of quick stories about his journey to winning the World Championship of Public Speaking. Then he threw out a few hints (or hooks) at what he could cover in the time available and threw the floor open.

The next forty-five minutes were made up of impromptu Q&A, and the value to the audience was extraordinary because they got to hear exactly what they wanted to. Not only that, but Mark's delivery style was fresh and spontaneous – necessarily so, because it was impromptu – which meant that the atmosphere in the room was electric. It was live, real, authentic, honest, unplugged, fast-paced and thrilling.

I remember that particular session to this day, many years later.

The cautionary note on using this technique is fairly obvious: don't attempt it if you haven't studied your stuff like a hybrid of nerd and Vulcan.

Mark Brown can use this approach because he is a world champion on his topic. He's not going to be asked a question that he can't answer, and answer masterfully. But, if you do know your stuff, this technique can solve a number of problems:

- It can refresh your own speaking, which may have become bogged down in repetitive 'same again' presentations.
- It can solve a problem with timing constraints if you are asked to speak at short notice, because – using this completely free-form technique –

you can speak to absolutely any time specifications you, the conference convenor or MC, may desire.

- It can draw new material from you, as you are forced to think about topics and angles on topics that you may not otherwise have considered. This can lead to some excellent new material for future presentations, as your audience tells you directly what they would actually like to hear about.

I have used this technique on a number of occasions, and each time I've come away thinking, 'That one bit was quite good. I'm going to add it to my prepared presentation and use it again in future.'

Start by introducing the topic in a compelling way, then throw out mental hooks, which subtly guide the audience in terms of what they might ask. Then open the floor and let the magic begin.

14. Facilitate a discussion

This technique is similar to co-creating with your audience, but it differs in the sense that you are not necessarily the expert, and you are not really facilitating a Q&A session in which you are obliged to give all the answers. Instead, you are introducing the topic and providing a forum for them to answer.

This technique does take a great deal of pressure off you as the speaker, but it also subtly changes your role. Use it if you genuinely want group input and discussion. But if you have been asked to deliver a full-scale presentation, be wary of using this. It could be seen as a cop-out.

I can think of at least three occasions (at major conventions) when speakers who were supposed to present useful information on a certain topic opted instead to host a facilitated discussion. I can tell you that the convenors were not amused!

In the right circumstances, though, it can be valuable.

This technique demands that you exercise a little bit of strength and show some useful degree of insight into the topic being discussed. You then lead the discussion in such a way that you give each person a fair amount of airtime – shutting them down tactfully when they go on too long, or drawing them out if they are shy and reluctant to contribute.

One similarity this technique shares with co-creating is that you need to throw out the right mental hooks. You need to lead their thinking in the right direction. You might actually say that the art in doing this correctly is simply knowing how to ask the right questions.

I can think of a very specific, real-world scenario in which I used this technique, in conjunction with a few others. I was asked to be the guest speaker at a strategic breakaway session for a mining company. On this occasion, however, I was asked to go slightly further than my usual sixty-minute keynote presentation. They asked me to facilitate a workshop session afterwards (based on my presentation), allowing them to engage in debate and discussion about how to practically use the principles in their own scenario.

I know next to nothing about how to manage a mining company. But I do understand principles of leadership, management and entrepreneurship. Based on this knowledge, and a little research beforehand, I was able to facilitate a discussion by simply asking the right questions. My keynote set the stage by inspiring strategic thinking, and the facilitation session afterwards gave them the opportunity to discuss how to implement some of the ideas directly into their scenario.

Interestingly, I have since started offering this format as part of my services as a professional speaker. There appears to be a big demand for it. Most of my speech topics now include the option of adding a two-hour workshop to the package, for an additional fee. When time permits, this option is quite popular at conferences. It is especially popular among small groups of management staff at strategic getaways. They want to get the full value out of an external speaker, and this is one way in which you can give extra value: knowing how to ask the right questions.

In my case, for instance, I might speak on the topic of innovation. During the workshop afterwards, I would then revisit one of the principles that I covered, and ask, 'How could you apply this idea in the marketing department?' or 'What would be the cost of allowing your competitors to implement such an idea first?'

So, this becomes another alternative to PowerPoint. Slides in the background are actually a hindrance in this scenario. They add nothing. The group dynamic is everything here.

To add a little additional skill and polish to your facilitation, think of each question that you ask as a mini speech. Introduce it by telling a story, or giving a vivid example. Raise some contrasting viewpoints around it. Pose the question, and then open the floor.

Once you determine that the discussion has run its course and it's time to move on to the next question (which may take longer than you originally anticipate – people tend to really get stuck in if you introduce the topic in a compelling way), you then regain control of the floor, and launch into your next mini speech. You introduce the next idea, tell another story and throw it open for debate once again.

Given that you are essentially playing the role of MC, do also be mindful of time. Make sure that you wrap up when you are supposed to.

15. Hint and reveal

With this, we have arrived at the last of my suggested structures that can replace PowerPoint. I have listed this particular structure last – and placed it right before Part 2, which focuses on props and visual aids – because this suggestion contains elements of both. It is at once a speech structure and an opportunity to use a prop to clever effect.

'Hint and reveal' is simple. You begin by hyping up the wonderful qualities of an object or idea, but only reveal what it is towards the end. It's a case of creating excitement with a series of mini promises, and then delivering on those promises with the revelation.

Over the course of a presentation, your speech would essentially be a sales pitch, focusing on everything that is to be gained from the item, or from the idea, which has yet to be revealed. You might say things like: 'This will revolutionise your life. Once you try it, you'll never go back' and various additional salesy schmaltz, before finally arriving at, 'And here it is!'

Naturally, you can see how props would also come into play when using such a technique. It is much more effective to take out and reveal a physical item than it is to simply talk it up descriptively without showing anything.

A trick to bear in mind: it's not just about the object you reveal. Your means of hiding it in the first place is important too. Very simple hide-

and-reveal catalysts work well for this structure – a box with a lid; a suitcase that you can open; cloth draped over the object – anything that is easy to wield and out of which, or from behind which, you can pull your 'rabbit', with a measure of theatricality.

You can probably already tell that this structure has limited application, but that it is particularly good at its one purpose, which is to build anticipation and then deliver on a promise. Because of this, it works well when selling a new idea or introducing a new thing in a favourable light. In particular, it works well when the new idea or thing is not up for debate. You are simply trying to create buy-in.

A classic scenario in which it might prove ideal would be the launch of a new car. You've seen it before. The vehicle is talked up in emotive terms and then finally revealed with a flourish (usually accompanied by flashing lights, loud music and scantily clad ladies).

Car designers with a good sense of theatre might even backlight the car behind a slightly translucent curtain, throwing its contours onto the fabric like an enticing shadow puppet. Tease and reveal benefits from large amounts of tease. The speaker espouses the many merits of the new design and then … *voila!* … reveals it with a flourish. Think of how disappointing and anti-climactic it would be to do it the other way around. The build-up is everything.

Another hypothetical scenario might be the in-house reveal of a new product to staff. The task is to build excitement to elicit buy-in. Therefore, a product launch is the perfect place to use this technique.

Naturally, you don't simply have to follow a rigid 'sell-then-reveal' structure. You can also split your speech into two, hyping up the new thing right to the point of revealing it, then speaking further about it after you have revealed it. In such a case, the logical approach would tend to be emotive, sales-orientated language in the first section, followed by technical explanations and specifications in the second section.

This is by no means a rule, though. It's simply a logical way of going about it.

And with this, we have arrived at the end of our section on structures that replace PowerPoint. Now let's move on to Part 2 and talk about toys!

PART 2

PROPS AND VISUAL AIDS THAT REPLACE THE NEED FOR SLIDES

Welcome to Part 2, in which we look at the physical props, toys and technology that can be used in place of PowerPoint. Some of these visual aids are fairly simple objects that get the job done in a basic way. Basic, however, can be extremely effective.

Others are more complex theatrical notions that can be employed to make your points and ideas spring vibrantly to life – like use of space and time, or staging that guides perception. Some are subtle, some are spectacular, some are very simple. All are alternatives to PowerPoint, and if you love speaking and presenting as much as I do, you'll see them as something of a treasure chest – an exciting collection of new goodies and gizmos with which you can experiment and play.

Try them together. Try them separately. Try them in the bathtub when no one is looking. Above all, enjoy using them. Your joy matters. A speaker can get away with a multitude of mistakes if he or she is genuinely enjoying the act of presenting. And these alternatives to PowerPoint can be used with such creativity that they add a whole new element of fun, not only for the audience, but also to your life and presenting career.

I hope you will love playing with these concepts every bit as much as I do.

As with the set of structures in Part 1, you can pick and choose between sections arbitrarily. However, you will gain the most value by a consecutive run-through of the ideas, as many of them build on the ones that come before. And, again, use one technique in isolation or combine a creative handful of them. I will point out certain obvious opportunities to mix and match as we go along.

Let's jump right in ...

16. Use an autocue

Why memorise an entire script when you can act like a politician and read it off a screen? If it works for Obama, why shouldn't it work for you?

Using a teleprompter or autocue sounds like cheating, doesn't it? As if it's somehow impure.

Perhaps the best way to look at it is to place the audience's benefit first. If your use of a teleprompter means that they get the full benefit of the things you intended to say, in word-perfect fashion, then so be it. Their benefit reigns supreme and should always be the central deciding factor.

Autocues perform a very similar function to PowerPoint, but they are superior in a number of ways. For instance, you get access to your full script without your audience seeing even keywords, as they would with slides. To all appearances, you are simply speaking naturally, not referring to notes at all, and your wording is perfect.

Most people tend to use PowerPoint as a form of cue card for their own benefit, and not as a form of visual aid for the audience's benefit. If that's you, then what you really need is an autocue, not slides. You crave reminders, and that's fine. Just don't convince yourself that the only valid form of reminder is PowerPoint. It isn't.

Here's another way in which autocues are superior to PowerPoint: an autocue is generally placed right in front of you at the foot of the stage, or directly before you at the back of the room, which means that you don't have to turn your head and lose the connection with your audience.

An automated teleprompter, which simply rolls at a set pace, is playing with fire. I wouldn't recommend it unless you have the opportunity to rehearse many times and you are absolutely sure that you can deliver that text, at that pace, without error. It's much better if you are able to control the pace of the scrolling text, or if someone you trust watches you and adjusts it as you go.

Some conference venues have autocues built into their infrastructure, ready to be used when you arrive.

Alternatively, you could use a smart device. There are apps like the Teleprompt for iPad, which are sophisticated enough to display your text while also recording a video of you presenting. This can be quite useful. It gives you the opportunity to review your presentation afterwards. It also makes it possible to upload your video to YouTube, or, depending on the quality you get, even turn it into a product, such as a DVD, that can be sold later. Just make sure that you have some way of mounting it. Placing it down by your feet will mean breaking eye contact with the audience. A best-case scenario would be some form of stand, placed centrally and roughly at eye level, without obstructing the audience's view of you.

You could even use the video as a form of value-add for the delegates – providing it to them in place of notes afterwards, either on disk, or as a downloadable link.

A tip for using autocues: when you are reading from a script, the writing style requires some degree of skill. Specifically, you need to be able to write a script that sounds like spoken language, rather than written language. Remember at the beginning of the book, when we spoke about telesales people who sound like they are reading to you? The real skill here lies in writing a script that does not sound written, but rather sounds like real speech. Spoken words tend to be less formal and tend to make use of shorter sentence structures.

It's easy enough to develop this skill if you're willing to put in the effort. It's a simple matter of writing the script, and then reading it out loud a couple of times. As you read it out loud, listen to yourself: do you sound natural?

Use abbreviations as well. In spoken language, people rarely use a phrase like 'It is true'. Instead, they will say, 'It's true.' Strive to sound as natural as possible. Write for the ear.

Use the poor man's autocue

The poor man man's autocue? *Was ist das?*

iPads are expensive. Not every venue has a built-in teleprompter. The poor man's autocue is quite simply any visual prompt that keeps you on track without distracting the audience or drawing attention to itself. You like the flying text from *Star Wars*? Why, with a little creative thinking, you can be your very own George Lucas!

As a simple example, you might stick a page to the back wall of the room, with four or five keywords printed in large lettering on it. You would then use each keyword to remind yourself of the major sections of your speech and keep you on track. A whiteboard discreetly positioned at the back of the room, or near the front and facing the stage, would achieve the same function. Essentially, you would be using cue cards without ever showing your cue cards.

The trick here is to make sure that the notes are as discreet as possible, and not to stare at them so obviously that the audience turns to see what you're reading. Simply glance at a keyword, resume eye contact with your audience and begin speaking on that idea.

If you're worried about people seeing your notes and perceiving this approach as amateurish, go ahead and disguise your notes. Don't use words at all. Use meaningful visuals: little mnemonic reminders of concepts. Let's say that you are addressing your staff and your three major points are:

1. an important deadline is now looming;
2. Sue is being promoted to head of sales; and
3. representatives from the media will be visiting the premises on Friday.

You could remember these points by tacking a page to the rear wall with:
1. a drawing of a wave looming over a surfer;
2. the word 'sales'; and
3. a drawing of a camera.

Naturally, there is a chance you'll draw a complete blank and tell your staff that a surfing tournament is looming, so they should all sell their cameras. But short of such an outright disaster, this technique generally works very well.

Or just use the room

You could even ditch the paper approach entirely and use physical objects instead. You might remind yourself to speak about filling in tax returns by leaving a coin on the table, or if you're feeling terribly clever indeed, you might turn the venue itself into a living mind map in which the lights above remind you about one point, while the glass of water on the table reminds you of another.

Don't get too abstract, though, because pressure tends to change things. The simpler and clearer your reminders are, the better.

Either way, the principle remains: what you really require is a set of reminders. And anything can be a reminder.

17. Use a prop

We have finally arrived at the classic, iconic, screamingly obvious replacement to PowerPoint slides. Yes, it's the simple, physical, pick-it-up prop. The curiosity that you hold up and show. The object. The item. The article. The artefact. The *thing*.

Like show-and-tell for grown-ups, props are more powerful than slides for the same reason that writing on a chart is. It's real, live, tactile and unusual. It's 3-D, and it's psychologically reminiscent of the hunter who returns to his clan, squats by the fireside as they all stare in wonder, and takes out the *thing* he found somewhere on the plains, turning it around in his hands to show them. Whip it out and watch the clan go, 'Ooooh!'

Naturally, the moment of revelation is key. That's where the magic lies, and it must be carefully managed.

An attractive prop, left lying on a display table as your audience files into the room, could be a distraction before you get to your point. An attractive prop, revealed and then placed back on the table, remains a distraction after you've made your point

To use a prop effectively, you should reveal it when it matters, then make it disappear from sight. You need to pull your rabbit out of a hat and then make it disappear again. Don't leave the rabbit running around the auditorium.

Of course, an attractive prop left on display under a cover, as discussed in the previous point about 'Hint and reveal', can be a great generator of excitement, although it too runs some risk of creating distraction.

Here are some logistics to consider when using a physical prop:
• Make sure that you have a way of getting the prop into the room

without it being seen beforehand. It spoils the moment of revelation if they saw you carry your brass tuba into the room earlier on.

- Make sure that it is well hidden before you begin, but in a place that allows you quick and fuss-free access. Alternatively, leave it on display, but covered for the big reveal.
- Do a dry run beforehand, in which you practise actually revealing and talking about your prop. You would be amazed how many small, awkward things can happen when you haven't tried it out first: the cover catches on a chair; it's too heavy to lift by yourself; you discover that the power cord won't reach the place where you had hoped to display it … silly little things like that, all of which are impossible to foresee without a rehearsal. Handling errors are easily resolved if you take the time and trouble to practise the prop segment of your speech beforehand.
- Once your prop is out and on duty, don't talk to it. Talk to your audience. Your prop is still only a visual aid that helps you to make your point. Your connection with the audience continues to be the most important part.
- If necessary, enlist help. There is a reason why game-show hosts of yore had the ubiquitous bikini babe to show the fridge. Aside from the obvious visual appeal, it's much easier to have another person to help you display your prop. This can free you up to present, and can free your hands up for gesturing, holding a microphone, etc. And that doesn't apply just to the part where you are doing the live delivery. Have someone help you carry it from your car and set it up in the room. It's preferable not to be a sweaty, soggy mess of a suit by the time you present.

The new technology of 3-D printers has added an entirely new dimension to props and their potential for use in your presentations.

Although not everyone has access to this relatively expensive form of technology, where it is available, its applications are as boundless as your creativity. You can print out mini models of an architectural design; you can print out actual replicas of what your finished product will look like; you can make the experience tactile for the audience by allowing them to touch and play with a beautiful, true-life rendering of the idea that you are speaking about.

The value to you, as the presenter, is in being able to make absolutely anything *visual* for an audience.

Without access to a 3-D printer, you can nevertheless make use of a prop without it even having to be a perfect replica for your idea. As a silly example, let's say that you were talking about the VW Beetle that your parents gave you when you went off to university. You could take out and hold up a small model of a Lamborghini. The humorous effect of the contradiction could be memorable in and of itself.

But it needn't be a glaringly discordant prop. You could, for instance, use a small, iconic representation to stand for a bigger idea, such as using a small, plastic soldier to speak about war, a globe of the world to speak about travel, or a goldfish in a bowl to speak about marine life.

Your use of props can also be more complex and nuanced than a single, simple item. For instance, you could set out a series of elaborate food dishes as you speak about the culinary norms of another nation, or you could hold up parts of a complex machine to show how they physically interact with one another.

All told, the advantage of a physical prop is simply the fact that people can look at an actual thing, rather than a visual representation on a screen. Also, they might have the opportunity to touch or interact with the prop, which leads us to our next idea …

18. Use interactive props

Now, let's take the idea of a basic prop one step further.

The simplest prop is a mere visual aid. You show it and nothing more. Its only role is to be placed there and be seen. *Ka-doonk* … 'Yay!'

But you can also make your props interactive. You can get members of the audience to do creative and interesting things with your props, whether it is to assemble parts, display them at different places in the room, wave them, throw them, catch them, fold them, cut them, cook them or stick them to the walls with silly putty.

People become more involved in your presentations when they get to tinker with something. Curiously, they even feel like they're being spoilt a little if they get to pick it up, hold it and play with it (whatever it might be). Once again, though, you need to follow some guidelines here:

- Make sure you can get the items into the room unnoticed, preferably beforehand.
- Make sure that the process of getting the item to the audience members is quick and slick. You don't want twenty minutes to go by while you personally hand a doodad to each person. This dynamic, if not properly handled, can chew up your presenting time. I've witnessed a twenty-minute presentation that went on for almost forty because the presenter started by giving handouts to the audience – a process that took a full twenty minutes.
- Make sure you lead your audience firmly and clearly. If your goal is to have them go through a certain process with their item, you don't want to lose control of the room and end up with a stockyard full of giggling monkeys randomly hurling bananas. Keep it to a guided tour.
- Be clear about whether or not they may keep their item, or what you want them to do with it afterwards. Lead them through the process with precise instructions. Don't leave any room for what might become an embarrassing misunderstanding.

May I have a volunteer?

You don't have to have one prop per audience member. You could just get one person to interact with your prop while the audience watches. The rest of the audience will buy into that one person's experience. They will empathise with them, laugh along with them, encourage them and experience it through their eyes.

I sometimes use a simple but effective technique to make a point about how, in human psychology, we have a tendency to make up restrictions that then hold us back in life. We favour rules over goals. This example generally features in my Rules of Hamster Thinking speech, and it goes like this: I ask for a volunteer from the audience (whom I might also incentivise with the opportunity to win one of my books). I then hand them a ball and place a piece of string directly in front of their feet. I then walk away from them, and head to the far side of the room, where I place a small bowl on the floor. At this point, I issue my instructions: 'Your goal is to get the ball into the bowl on the count of three. One, two, three … Go!'

Predictably, what happens next is that the delegate will try to throw the ball across the room and into the bowl. It is impossible. Even if your aim were that good, the ball would knock the bowl over.

The answer, of course, is to simply step over the piece of string, walk to the bowl and place the ball in it. I never said that they had to remain behind the piece of string. I never said that they were supposed to throw it. My only instruction was: 'Get the ball into the bowl.'

This simple illustration is very effective in making the point about how we deduce rules where there aren't any, make assumptions that can hinder our performance and prefer to think within safe systems of behaviour, rather than being ruthlessly efficient at reaching our goals. I make the point that, often, the negative belief itself is the only real restriction.

When I use this illustration, I usually give the volunteer two or three chances. By the time they've thrown the ball twice, they either catch on by themselves, or members of the audience start shouting, 'Just walk over!' Interestingly, the delegate will then typically look at me for permission, which helps to make my point. I simply shrug.

Eventually, the delegate will succeed – walking over and placing the ball in the bowl. This is good from the perspective that I don't simply embarrass the delegate. They get the opportunity to be seen overcoming the challenge and winning their prize, which is definitely preferable.

I then extrapolate from what the audience has just seen to how we all do the same thing, in different situations – once again, being careful to show that this sort of thinking applies to everyone, myself included – and that I'm not just picking on my volunteer.

Then I go on to speak for the next fifty minutes or so about how large corporate companies make up restrictive, culture-based rules that actually work against their own goals and how, as individuals, we tend to place methodology ahead of results.

So, why go to all this trouble? I could simply spend thirty seconds explaining, conceptually, that humans often favour rules over goals. Wouldn't that be more efficient? The answer is, yes, but it would be much less effective and much less memorable.

My whole presentation centres on the audience really getting that one idea and taking it to heart. For that reason, I want to belabour it, illustrate it, draw it out, make it visual, get them to interact with it and really drive the concept home. As a result of their participation in the experiment, they will truly believe that humans favour rules over goals. That's a world apart from simply being told that it is the case.

Play time

You can be even cleverer than that. Why have each member of the audience playing with their own prop, or just one member of the audience interacting with a prop, when you can get multiple members to interact with each other's props? (Sounds like the sixties, doesn't it?)

'Bob, you have a gizmo. Janet, seated over there, has a thingamabob. Take your gizmo and see if you can get it to work with Janet's thingamabob.'

Brilliant!

Interactive props are great for humour, playfulness, interaction and psychological buy-in. They are adept at illustrating a technical message, but they really come into their own when your goals are more about team dynamics and creating a good vibe in the room. (Note: if the final product is something surprising, and/or visually clever – for instance, the combined parts surprise the audience by making up their own brand logo … you may even generate applause.)

The trick with carrying out this technique is to really think it through from one end to the other. What happens when they do this? Once they're done, what happens next? Do I just say 'thank you' and it's over? Or is there some smoother way of transitioning into the next phase of my presentation, or the next item on the meeting's agenda? Where do the bits and bobs go? Do they hand them back to me? Do they just put them down on the floor?

Think it through, plan it thoroughly and, if possible, rehearse it as far as is feasible.

Once again, having an assistant to help you with the logistics will make life much easier for you, and might make the presentation itself seem even more professional.

19. Carry out a display

Like to create a little drama? Work a little visual voodoo? Make them say 'Oooh' and 'Aaah'? Use a prop that *does* something. Use a display of a process, or a reactive agent that goes through a process.

By way of example, you could mix different colours of dyed water; melt something so that it drips, pours and runs; heat up kernels until they pop into popcorn ... anything that goes through a physical process.

Displays are extremely powerful. They take the hypothetical (which might not penetrate human cynicism) and make it real for that audience. Displays lend perspective.

I recall an episode of the television show *Airport 24/7: Miami*, in which the airport's head of safety took his staff out to an open field and detonated an actual shoe bomb in front of them. Their facial expressions, upon seeing the devastation, were priceless. After the detonation, he simply concluded with the line, 'Any questions why our passengers should take their shoes off?'

One of the staff was then filmed saying: 'After experiencing an explosive demonstration, it puts you in a little more perspective. The sight, the light, the sound, the boom and the vibrations and the shockwave that hit you. It's actually very intense. I'm gonna look at everything with a new set of eyes now.'

You too can take the mundane and make your audience look at it with a new set of eyes by using a demonstration.

From the audience's perspective, a demonstration can be almost hypnotic to watch. It's like a mini physics display, performed as part of a presentation. They can hardly fail to gawp at the baking-soda volcano as it erupts to crazy proportions.

This is a high-input technique. It requires planning and logistics on your part, but the pay-off can be worth the input.

Here is a very simplified example to illustrate how the display technique might be used. Let's say that two teams in a company are being merged together, and the speaker – their new manager – is trying to inspire them to pool their different skills and traits, and get along.

She might use a bowl of water and add one colour of dye to illustrate the first team, then add a different colour to illustrate the second team.

The pay-off from this illustration would be how the combined colours mix to create a brand-new colour in the bowl. Yay! Hurray!

From this very simplified illustration, you can probably also deduce the importance of practising with your props beforehand. If you do, and you get the amounts just right, you may dazzle and impress your audience when you finally present your experiment live. If you try it for the first time live in front of them, and the colours combine to create a swampy, muddy hue, which then becomes sentient and wanders off looking for food, you will most likely make up for it by turning a spectacular shade of red yourself.

Also, you need to know in advance how messy it might be. Don't assume your baking-soda volcano will pour down the side of the table, collecting neatly on the little towel you placed below, when in fact it's going to hit the rafters and disperse lava in a SeaWorld-like splash zone.

Naturally, and perhaps obviously, you should also ensure that you don't injure any of your audience members while doing your display. Setting delegates on fire, or sending your boss into an alternate dimension, will not earn you brownie points.

Always practise before presenting it live. This principle holds for any presentation that you do.

Ultimately, the greater the visual drama you can create, the better your display will be. If your display includes a clear visual change – something transitioning from one state to another – it will be highly memorable. And don't discount the psychological impact of appealing to the other senses as well: smell, taste, touch and sound.

20. Break something

That's right. Break something. Go Greek! Throw that plate and shout your hearty, 'Opa!' Why shouldn't you?

Why should you? Because people in conferences do not expect to see something broken. Formally dressed, in attendance at an event with certain accepted social norms, they expect to sit in semi-darkness and see reams of mind-numbing PowerPoint slides from the safety of their comfort zones. They expect conference behaviour. So surprise them. The impact can be tremendous.

Your audience members are in a certain social behavioural mode and, for that reason, when you take out a dish or a plank, a vase or a light-bulb, a balloon or a long-playing gramophone that once belonged to your beloved Aunt Martha and break it spectacularly against a pillar, smash it loudly on the ground, pop it theatrically with a pin or pound it vigorously with a hammer (this one's quite satisfying) – the impact is meteoric.

At the heart of this technique is simple shock value. And that means that we are walking a fine line with this technique. Good taste is on one side and shocking just for the sake of being shocking is on the other.

I believe that the guiding principle for this technique should be this: does it add something to your presentation? Does it help you to communicate your idea and your message? If not, you may just be doing it for your own benefit.

But if it does, boy oh boy, you have one of the world's greatest attention grabbers in your oratory arsenal!

It makes a particularly good opener. If you choose to go this route, you might even opt to walk on stage in silence and – without greeting the audience – start by breaking your object.

I once used this technique in a contest-winning speech for Toastmasters. The speech was titled Look at Me! and its theme was the exploration of how people validate one another in relationships. I referred to *Shall We Dance?*, a movie featuring Richard Gere and Susan Sarandon, in which Sarandon's character explains why humans need relationships. 'We need a witness to our lives,' she says, in a touching little speech to a cynical private eye who is asking why she thinks people ever bother to get together in the first place.

To add a little theatricality to my delivery, I opened my speech by walking onto the stage in silence. There (set up in advance) was a small table, with a single champagne glass, standing atop a silk napkin. After a few moments of eye contact with the audience, I turned and picked up the glass, examined it for a second, then wrapped it in the napkin. I then lowered it to the floor, and – acting out a Jewish wedding tradition – stomped on it.

This got an excellent reaction from the audience, whom I then addressed for the first time with my opening line, 'Why do people marry? Why do we bother to get together?'

The theatrical effect was excellent, although I can tell you that it takes a little courage to start with a bit of theatre carried out in silence. You, as the presenter, will be profoundly aware of the tension around the room. But that's the point, isn't it? Create tension. Grab attention. Hook their interest from the word 'go'.

As a quick aside, I used the broken champagne glass again later in the same speech. I was referring to broken hearts and broken lives, and all I did was kneel beside the napkin, open it gently and take out a single shard of broken glass. I held it up and spoke my lines while looking at the shard. Then I dropped it gently back into the napkin and carried on speaking.

In public-speaking terminology, and in the terminology of comedians, this is called a throwback. It may also be referred to as a callback. Both terms mean the same thing. It's simply the art of referencing something that came before. It can look very slick – it can also have excellent humour value.

Breaking an object: the more unlikely the person who does it, the more effective the technique. If buttoned down, prim, proper and conservative, moustachioed old Stephen, the head of accounts, is expected to be boring every time he talks, Stephen could do well to shake things up by breaking something.

Also, the more formal the occasion, the greater the effect.

This is not to say that it won't work if Jay, the spiky-haired, tattooed maverick from the advertising department, does it at a lunchtime rally. But, certainly, the effect is amplified exponentially in the hands of Stephen, in a formal setting.

Here, again, do plan your logistics in advance. In the case of the Toastmasters conference, I had an assistant carry the table, napkin and glass up onto the stage before my presentation, and then remove them afterwards. The same assistant was armed with a small brush and dustpan, in case any of the shards of glass escaped. Cleaning up that sort of thing is your responsibility as the presenter.

21. Put it where they'll least expect it

Most singers simply walk onto the stage and begin belting out their hits. But, from time to time, you will encounter someone who is more than just a singer: a unique individual who is a *performer*. Pop star Robbie Williams is one such creature.

In his famous Live at Knebworth concert, Robbie made his entrance on stage suspended upside down from a rope below a hovering helicopter. You can imagine this would have generated quite a reaction.

Why not try that in your next boardroom presentation?

Okay, perhaps that's a tad overkill. But breaking norms and doing the unexpected is always extremely powerful. That, really, is the premise of this entire book: don't do what everyone else does. Don't do the expected. Surprise them with creativity. Be unique.

So, let's bring that principle down to simpler levels and see how we can apply it to our scenario as speakers.

You can bring additional vibrancy to a visual aid simply by placing it somewhere unexpected. Playing on the notion that audiences are anticipating 'normal conference behaviour' – place your visual aids somewhere that your delegates do not expect to see them.

What is the standard practice? On the stage (or at the front of the boardroom) ... in the middle. Same as everyone else in the history of dull presenting.

By contrast, you might make your reasonably boring doohickey look quite spectacular by placing it on top of a pillar and lighting it from above. If nothing else, you may achieve a certain amount of humour.

But don't limit yourself to the stage, or to the front of the room. Sometimes the best way to hide something is in plain view. Could you draw it on the floor beneath their feet, then invite them to remove their chairs, come up to the stage en masse, and observe how the whole room is now the diagram you are presenting to them? Could you hide it on the ceiling? Could you hide it among them on a specific seat?

The very act of placing a prop in an unusual setting draws attention to it and forces the audience to think of it in a new, novel light.

If your prop is big (and mobile), you might have someone wheel it in through the rear doors – to pomp and fanfare – at just the right moment so that your audience has to turn to watch its grand Roman parade-style arrival. This gives you the opportunity for a dramatic, television courtroom-style gesture towards the back of the room: 'Here comes the real killer now!'

Do make sure that whoever is supposed to bring it in does it on cue, though. There's nothing more anticlimactic and oddly hilarious than a dramatic gesture towards a door where, all of a sudden, nothing happens!

Because this technique relies on the specific environment in which you will be speaking, go to the venue and do some creative dreaming. Look around. What can you use? Where can you put things? Be guided by the simple principle, what would be extremely cool?

You can even go so far as to think outside the parameters of the room itself. For instance, could something be placed just outside a window within easy reach? Or how about in the ceiling? Imagine the effect of walking up a ladder, pushing aside a ceiling panel, and bringing down a prop. Your audience would never forget that sort of novelty.

The note of caution if you adopt this technique is a strange one: make sure that the cleaners don't clear away your prop! I've seen this happen. Also, work in conjunction with the conference convenors and/or the people in charge of the venue itself. It's surprising how often a well-meaning venue employee will see an oddity and clear it away, just in time for your spectacular unveiling. Your presentation will not benefit from the words, 'Sorry, folks. Give us a few minutes while we search the premises for my prop.'

22. Play video

The human race is increasingly using video as a primary means of consuming ideas and content. We watch the news, we entertain ourselves by viewing movies and we download thought-provoking speeches, entertaining comedy and video clips of adorable kittens. Perhaps my next book will be *50 Ways to Amuse Your Brain Without Video*.

Video presents some similar problems to PowerPoint. You will still need a projector, a power source and a DVD player or laptop. You will still require the same preparation time, the same set-up time on the day, and you still face the same danger of the equipment fighting back. It's a comical but all too common sight to see a presenter proudly clicking the play button and standing back dramatically, expecting a video clip to wow and mesmerise, only to have their laptop stare at them like a lobotomised sheep.

But, for now, putting your ideas into video format remains an effective technique. In terms of benefits, video can help you show a great deal of information very quickly. It's flashy and entertaining, and aside from the dramatic effect of good visuals, there is also the efficiency of being able to show interviews with people not present; footage of venues; time-lapse sequences of things being built; fly-throughs and much, much more.

Video achieves a great deal in a short space of time.

Professional speaker Brian Walter often says, 'Use Hollywood's budget. They've invested millions in getting that scene to convey an idea. Use their production value.'

Of course, you do need to pay licensing rights to do this honestly, but the cost is not always prohibitive. Unfortunately, it's easier to do this in the United States than elsewhere. If you are US-based, you can go to www.mplc.org to retain a service that will allow you to legally license the use of movie and some television clips in your speeches. Other countries would require a Google search along the lines of 'licensing of video footage for public viewing'.

Alternatively, you can shoot your own footage. Just make sure you know what you're doing, though. Anything that you film should be properly lit, shot using a reasonably high-definition device, and should have good sound. It will also need some editing afterwards.

In a best-case (albeit expensive) scenario, you can hire a professional cameraman, or an entire production crew, to shoot your original video for you.

Not the same as PowerPoint?

Although it is true that you can show a video clip within a PowerPoint presentation, I separate video out because it is in fact quite different.

PowerPoint requires you to speak while a slide is being shown, therefore making it a background effect to you, and often something of a distraction. Video is different, in the sense that it stands alone. You generally do not speak while showing it. You stop speaking and then you play the video. The video then performs its own, unique function. It is a break from speaking, allowing you a moment of respite while the on-screen visuals continue to achieve your objectives.

I am not a fan of embedding video in PowerPoint because embedded video is like a great cosmic vacuum that draws the potential for errors from distant galaxies towards it. I think it's safe to say that the number one technical glitch at conferences around the world occurs when a speaker tries to play a video clip embedded in a PowerPoint presentation. I think it is also fair to say that I have seen this fail more often than I have seen it work successfully. In other words, I've seen a higher rate of failure than of success. For this reason, it can be asking for trouble.

There are many ways in which you can use video. One of the cleverest uses of this medium I've ever seen was by South African humourist Gavin Sharples and his Celebrity Testimonial intro.

Gavin is never introduced by an MC. There is no need. His keynotes always open with the same video clip, which shows an assortment of A-list celebrities (Tom Cruise, Nicole Kidman, Steven Spielberg and many others) apparently talking about him. Of course, they weren't doing any such thing at the time; they were talking about their colleagues and associates in the film industry, in a series of unrelated interviews.

But with a little clever editing, the end result is that we see a clip of Gavin on stage, and then Tom Cruise saying, 'He's the best I've ever worked with.' Then more Gavin, and Penélope Cruz saying, 'He's just such an unbelievable talent. Almost superhuman.' Then more Gavin, then Archbishop Desmond Tutu singing his praises, and so on.

It never fails to delight audiences.

One lesson that I have picked up from watching this particular clip played at numerous venues, for different audiences, is that sound quality is of the utmost importance.

At one particular venue, the sound system had an inferior, tinny, echoey quality. As a result, the audience could see Tom Cruise, but they couldn't quite make out what he was saying. The effect, therefore, was lost, and it put Gavin at a disadvantage when he began, because not only had the humour failed to create rapport, but he had effectively had no introduction whatsoever. Fortunately, Gavin is a talent and he easily overcame this momentary setback.

It is also interesting to note how lateral this piece of theatricality is. It provides no real information. We are given no actual résumé, no legitimate background as to who or what Gavin is, and no clue regarding what we are about to experience. It's just pure entertainment. Its only purpose is to delight! But it puts the audience into a good mood, establishes rapport and, for that reason, it works like a charm. That's showbiz, baby!

In the National Speakers Association book *Paid to Speak*, we are told that a good intro doesn't have to be a biography. Instead, it should be '… a warm handshake with the audience'. Gavin's creative approach is precisely that.

Video can be used to make much more serious points, as well. In *Innovative Presentations for Dummies*, authors Ray Anthony and Barbara Boyd talk about the founder and CEO of a technology company. The CEO was faced with a difficult managerial decision that she had to make and then explain to the rest of the organisation.

Because she wanted to be seen as a caring and considerate leader, it was important to her to recreate her thought processes and show how deeply she had considered the various options when delivering her final decision to the company. The decision had significant consequences, and it took her weeks of toing and froing to make the call. But how could she convey that to the audience?

She decided not to use PowerPoint, believing it to be too impersonal. Instead, she had a professional video crew film her wearing two different outfits (one light and one dark) arguing back and forth with herself.

On the day, she sat between the two video versions of herself and became part of a live, interactive (and obviously highly rehearsed) three-way dialogue. In this manner, she was able to take the audience through the entire emotional journey of the decision, showing vividly that she understood the arguments both ways. As the authors comment:

> She could have taken the easy route and just done a quick summary of the sterile, analytical pros and cons, but she rehearsed this innovative presentation and the empathic, psychological effect on her managers and professionals was not just incredibly persuasive, but empathically spellbinding.

Talk about going to great lengths to get buy-in. Kudos to her!

If you plan to use video in your presentations, here are some guidelines:

- If you want to use someone else's video, make sure that you have the legal right to do so.
- If you want to obtain a licence for the legal right to show, for instance, part of a Hollywood blockbuster, you can make use of an agency that will sell you such rights. Use Hollywood's production value.
- If you are using your own footage, make sure it is competently shot.
- Make sure it is competently or even professionally edited, preferably down to the shortest possible time frame.
- Make sure that anyone who speaks on camera uses a lapel microphone, or that their speech is caught with an overhead microphone (or that they are at least close enough to the camera for the sound to be picked up on the camera's built-in microphone).
- Lighting is incredibly important. One of the surest signs of amateur video footage is an underlit scene.
- As with any other visual aid, test your video before trying it on a live audience (and with the actual equipment you will be using and in the actual venue where you will be using it).

23. Play music

Some professional speakers believe that it is advantageous to set the right emotional tone for their presentation by playing music as their audience is entering the room. Music can communicate mood and tone in ways that slides simply cannot. When did you last walk into a candlelit five-star restaurant and immediately realise that this would be a posh dining experience ... based on the slides?

Speakers will often go for something vibey like Bon Jovi's 'It's My life', 'Tonight's Going to be a Good Night' by the Black Eyed Peas, 'The Summer of '69' by Brian Adams, or any one of a plethora of upbeat anthems with that certain energy. AC/DC's 'Thunderstruck' remains a perennial favourite, as does Queen's 'We Will Rock You'. These songs are particularly suited to big rallies, and organisations often use them ahead of a big drive or campaign.

With a little creativity, music can highlight an idea just as effectively as a visual might. As a hypothetical example, imagine that your presentation is about three international venues that your entourage visited on a working tour, and the three big new technology ideas that you took away from each country.

You might play a few seconds of a traditional Irish jig, then fade the music and say, 'Touchdown in Dublin, where IT specialists have solved the very problem we've been wrestling with …'

After that, you may play a few bars of the German national anthem, fade the music and say, 'Deutschland next. And, in addition to some world-class sausage and beer, our hosts provided us with insightful technical expertise for our project.'

After that, you might play a few seconds of traditional Zulu drums, then announce, 'Down to southern Africa, where we wrapped up our tour at the convention centre in Johannesburg. The taxis were frightening.'

By using music this way, you have divided your presentation into three neat sections. Each instance of musical input creates and denotes its own segment, dividing your presentation into a pleasing rhythmic structure.

Not only that, but the music will also have helped to make your presentation come alive. It adds vibrancy and flavour, and shows a degree of concern for the audience's enjoyment. It says, 'I went to this trouble simply for your pleasure.' Small cues like that can go a long way towards winning an audience over. Remember, it's not just about the information: it's about the total impression you create, and going the extra mile in this manner creates a very favourable impression.

Music is an excellent scene-setter and because it is so rarely used its effect can be impactful. But it isn't limited to opening moments. You can also use music for humorous effect, perhaps playing 'The Imperial March' from *Star Wars* as the CEO takes to the front of the room, or (and this is a little tacky, but I've seen it done and it got a good reaction) 'I'm Too Sexy' when the groom stands up to speak at a wedding reception. It may not be original at this point, having been done at a million weddings around the world, but it can still get a giggle from the audience.

As a mood setter, climate creator and perceptions driver, music can help you make your point without PowerPoint. It excels in creating an emotional climate.

24. Play sound

You don't actually have to film somebody speaking to include their commentary in your presentation. You can just record their voice. The effect is sometimes more dramatic than video. It can elevate the sense of importance of what they are saying – denoting a lofty and grand status (if that is the impression you wish to communicate).

Imagine the effect when the disembodied voice of the corporation's international president booms over the speaker system in a dark auditorium – 'Greetings, minions!' – like Hannibal Lecter addressing Clarice out of the dark. Only marginally less frightening.

This technique can be used in other ways too. You are not limited to just voice recordings. You can use all manner of sound effects. If you were discussing famous disasters, and referenced the explosion of the Space Shuttle *Challenger*, the sound of the radio transmissions to the shuttle – beeps, bloops, crackles and all – could be exponentially more emotive than visuals. The same might apply with famous audio clips such as the radio broadcast of the *Hindenburg* disaster.

The human mind is acutely tuned in to voice. Our parents' voices were our primary source of learning and love and rebuke when we were infants, and our minds remain attuned to voice as a result.

A goodly number of thespians will still argue that storytelling reached its pinnacle during the days of radio drama. Theatre of the mind: a craft so agile, so vivid and unforgettably emotive made use of only a single medium: the human voice.

Entire books have been devoted to using the full range and expressive power of the human voice. Specialists worldwide make a living by coaching others in vocal technique, and public-speaking organisations like Toastmasters have assignments on vocal technique as part of their curriculum.

Sometimes it pays to think in very simple terms. Instead of bombarding the audience with visuals, how about turning off the lights and using only sound? How about reducing their sensory input to the single stimulus of sound?

This is a sterling example of less is more.

Of course, you needn't rely only upon pre-recorded sound. You can also create emotive sound live, which brings us to our next idea ...

25. Use live voice

In 2010, I published a book with my friend and colleague Tony Cross: *So You're in Charge, Now What? 52 Ways to Become a Better Leader*.

Tony and I often speak and train together, and it's a delight to work with him because he is immensely creative and always willing to try out strange and novel ideas. (This pertains only to speeches. We don't dress up in lingerie and chase one another.)

Tony and I have used live voice at two separate events. The first was a meeting of the United Professional Sales Association. To make a dramatic point, one of us hid in a side room with a microphone and, on cue, did a 'voice from heaven'.

We took the concept one step further, a couple of years later at a sales conference for information-storage company Metrofile.

For the Metrofile event, we prepared an entire scripted dialogue between myself on stage (as the speaker), and Tony hiding behind a curtain with a microphone. I have reproduced the entire script below. As you'll see, it plays on some insider jokes, which depend on the audience's knowledge of their own company, and of key personalities (including the character Guy) within the company.

The script, in isolation, doesn't look particularly funny. But the repartee between me and the disembodied voice worked wonderfully on the night. It went like this:

DOUGLAS: Welcome to the Metrofile Awards Evening! I'll be your host tonight.

DISEMBODIED VOICE: Doug! (Pause.) Douuug!

DOUGLAS: Yes?

DISEMBODIED VOICE: Before you begin …

DOUGLAS: Yes?

DISEMBODIED VOICE: How much do you actually know about Metrofile?

DOUGLAS: About Metrofile? Well, not much really. I mean, I know a guy …

DISEMBODIED VOICE: A guy?

DOUGLAS: Yes, Guy! So … what *does* Metrofile do?

DISEMBODIED VOICE: They keep your documents safe.

DOUGLAS: So, they help if I need a document?

DISEMBODIED VOICE: Yes.

DOUGLAS: How?

DISEMBODIED VOICE: By taking it away.

DOUGLAS: But what if I need it?

DISEMBODIED VOICE: Then they bring it back.

DOUGLAS: But what if the document is important?

DISEMBODIED VOICE: Then they'll take it away for you.

DOUGLAS: So, they take away my important documents?

DISEMBODIED VOICE: Yes.

DOUGLAS: Why?

DISEMBODIED VOICE: Because you need them.

DOUGLAS: What if I need them now?

DISEMBODIED VOICE: Then they'll bring them back.

DOUGLAS: So ... where do they keep them?

DISEMBODIED VOICE: Off-site.

DOUGLAS: Out of sight?

DISEMBODIED VOICE: No, in sight. Just *off*-site.

DOUGLAS: But what if I need them?

DISEMBODIED VOICE: Then they'll bring them back.

DOUGLAS: In sight?

DISEMBODIED VOICE: No, on-site.

DOUGLAS: So, how will they find them? Where they left them?

DISEMBODIED VOICE: Yes, off-site.

DOUGLAS: Okay, so when my important documents are out of sight, off-site, who's the guy in charge?

DISEMBODIED VOICE: No, not Guy. Graham.

DOUGLAS: So, Graham is the guy?

DISEMBODIED VOICE: No, Guy is the guy. Graham is in charge.

DOUGLAS: So, who's Guy?

DISEMBODIED VOICE: Graham is in charge of Guy.

DOUGLAS: So, what do they put my documents into?

DISEMBODIED VOICE: Boxes.

DOUGLAS: Boxes?

DISEMBODIED VOICE: Boxes. Brown boxes.

DOUGLAS: Brown boxes?

DISEMBODIED VOICE: Well, sometimes orange.

DOUGLAS: Orange boxes?

DISEMBODIED VOICE: And brown boxes.

DOUGLAS: So, orange and brown boxes?

DISEMBODIED VOICE: Yes.

DOUGLAS: Managed by Guy?

DISEMBODIED VOICE: No, Graham.

DOUGLAS: Managed by Graham, who's managed by Guy?

DISEMBODIED VOICE: Yes.

DOUGLAS: So Graham takes my important documents and stores them, off-site, out of sight until I need them?

DISEMBODIED VOICE: Yes.

DOUGLAS: And he brings them back?

DISEMBODIED VOICE: Yes.

DOUGLAS: In his car?

DISEMBODIED VOICE: No, in boxes.

DOUGLAS: In boxes?

DISEMBODIED VOICE: Yes, orange or brown boxes.

DOUGLAS: So, where are they housed?

DISEMBODIED VOICE: In a warehouse.

DOUGLAS: Where?

DISEMBODIED VOICE: House. Yes.

DOUGLAS: So, they're stored in some guy's warehouse?

DISEMBODIED VOICE: No, in Graham's.

DOUGLAS (Long pause.) Oh ...

DISEMBODIED VOICE: And sometimes they scan stuff.

DOUGLAS: What do they scan?

DISEMBODIED VOICE: The papers.

DOUGLAS: The papers in the boxes?

DISEMBODIED VOICE: Yes, the papers in the boxes in the warehouse, out of sight, off-site.

DOUGLAS: And then what do they do with the scans?

DISEMBODIED VOICE: Put them in CDs.

DOUGLAS: Seedy boxes?

DISEMBODIED VOICE: No.

DOUGLAS: Seedy cars?

DISEMBODIED VOICE: No. CDs.

DOUGLAS: Oh! CDs! So then, where do they put the CDs?

DISEMBODIED VOICE: In boxes. And then they put the boxes in the vault.

DOUGLAS: In the vault?

DISEMBODIED VOICE: Yes.

DOUGLAS: Like the banks?

DISEMBODIED VOICE: No, *for* the banks.

DOUGLAS: What if the banks need them?

DISEMBODIED VOICE: Then they bring them back.

DOUGLAS: In their cars?

DISEMBODIED VOICE: No in boxes. Orange ones.

DOUGLAS: Ah, I think I finally understand – they don't sell *boxes*: they sell *value*.

DISEMBODIED VOICE: Bingo, Douglas, bingo!

And that's how we launched the evening to (as we recall) loud and sustained applause. The degree of wackiness or drama is up to you, but the concept can be very effective.

If you do plan to use a back-and-forth discussion technique, you will need a lot of rehearsal. I will confess that I used a lectern for this one, so that I could have the exact script for the conversation right in front of me. To make it look real, and to avoid the appearance of reading a script, I would glance down and read as Tony's disembodied voice boomed over the speakers, then look up before delivering my own line.

26. Use a lectern and a script

The oldest (and arguably most classical) form of public speaking is to stand behind a lectern and refer to notes.

In many ways – with its overtones of an academic lecture – this approach can seem a little dated. It nevertheless has its merits, if adapted and used cleverly.

One of the facets that make it seem dated is the visual barrier that a lectern creates between the speaker and the audience. Watch a video of professional speakers from decades gone by (Leo Buscaglia springs to mind), and you will almost always see them standing behind a wooden lectern. Watch a speaker from the 2000s onward (think Steve Jobs or any of the famous TED Talks), and you will inevitably see a speaker on an open stage moving about freely: no lectern.

Conference convenors and venue owners have found a reasonably successful compromise with the introduction of transparent glass lecterns. This offers the best of both worlds: the presenter has a place for his or her notes and a glass of water, while the audience still has a full view of the speaker.

Personally, I have an absolute rule of thumb regarding lecterns: I never use them when delivering a speech, but I always use them when I'm MC at an event.

As an MC, I have to introduce speakers in some degree of detail. It's useful to have their titles directly before me, along with the specific names, for instance, of their books or well-known articles. Though these details are important, I always make a point to humanise their introductions (speakers will notoriously hand you a formal bio, which makes for a terrible introduction). Reading out a bio sounds awkward and overly formal. It wasn't designed to be read out loud, so it doesn't work in spoken form. The result is that the MC looks like he or she is 'stepping out' of natural speech mode to deliver the information. It reduces the energy of the evening.

I usually pick out four or five of the most pertinent facts and relate them to the audience in something of a story format: 'Janet sees the world differently from most people. As the author of *How to Sue Anyone for Bad Grammar*, she is waging a one-woman war on poor diction and clunky sentences. Janet has been honoured for her efforts by universities around the globe – one of which incurred her wrath by misspelling her name on a certificate. Today she will be sharing her top tips for a more eloquent world. Please help me to welcome Janet.'

I will then remain at the lectern while I wait for Janet to walk up. Only after I have shaken her hand will I take my seat again. This just looks professional.

Naturally, the biggest advantage of a lectern is that it allows you to have your notes right in front of you. I'd like to caution you, however, to really take the following thought to heart: this is also the lectern's biggest disadvantage!

By now, I've spent a fair amount of your time and my energy trying to convey the idea that the best speeches and presentations do not sound like written language read aloud. Take a lengthy, literary script up to the lectern and read it out loud: I guarantee that you will have a dreadful speech on your hands.

So, how do you get all the good without suffering the bad? For starters, turn the lectern to a three-quarter angle. Instead of hiding behind it, angle it so that you're essentially standing next to it. This will give you the advantage of being able to glance to the side at your notes, while also ensuring that the audience gets a full-frontal view (which is exciting under any circumstances).

Next, do not take a comprehensively written script along with you. Take keywords, or key points only. If you have to read and comprehend sentences, while you are busy with the separate skills of oratory delivery and emotional connection, one or the other will suffer. Generally, it tends to be oratory and the emotional connection. You simply can't be reading and processing, as well as connecting and delivering.

Instead, glance quickly and subtly down at your keyword, look up from it, re-establish eye contact, and deliver your thoughts with warmth and connection.

Another extremely useful trick, which I've mentioned before, is to use mind maps. Rather than writing words, draw small cartoon pictures that remind you of the concepts. Draw them in separate bubbles, with a line linking each thought to the next one. This will show you in a very 'quick to process' way what your current thought is, and how it leads on to the next one.

Another tip on using this technique: try not to stray too far away from the lectern. You don't want to reach the end of your particular thought, and then have to walk back (or even backwards) to where your notes are.

A skilful speaker can range around the stage or speaking area, and when he or she starts to conclude that particular section, will walk back to the lectern while wrapping up the thought – arriving back there in time to glance at the notes, with no awkward silence in between. But it does often happen that an inexperienced speaker will meander happily to the far side of the stage, run out of things to say and then awkwardly stumble back to the lectern, either in silence or accompanied by a winning phrase like, 'Um … Excuse me while I get back to my notes.'

You can also use a small table in place of a lectern, and I do this myself from time to time. I use this technique particularly if I am delivering a new presentation without slides, and need to remember my major points. I will take a small stand or table up on to the stage, place it off to one side and occasionally wander over to it for a quick glance at my notes. It's also useful if, for instance, you want to hold up a book or show a prop of some sort.

Another thought in passing: if you like to have water available (which I certainly do), don't take ice water up to the lectern. It can literally freeze your tongue and cause your diaphragm to tighten, which makes speaking a great deal harder, and the sounds coming out of your mouth a great deal more squeaky and comical. Instead, try to go for water that is at room temperature or, ideally, even a little warm. Warmth frees up and loosens all the muscles associated with making beautiful sounds that cause audiences to swoon. And why shouldn't you be the Josh Groban of your next office meeting?

The lectern remains a useful speaking tool, but make sure that its use is not conspicuous. Get the best out of it without showing dependence upon it. And, for heaven's sake, please don't grab onto the lectern like a life preserver. White knuckles do not portray sexy self-confidence. It's best not to have any physical contact with the lectern whatsoever. Stand boldly in your space and *own it*.

A final, logistical thought: lecterns are often used in settings where the lights are ultimately dimmed. This can catch speakers off guard. You've walked up to the lectern beforehand, placed your notes there, gone through a few confident rehearsals and you're feeling ready. Then the event begins – the lights go down and you can't see a thing. Some lecterns have built in, low-level lights, designed to solve this very problem. If yours has one, remember to switch it on in advance. If not, try to make provision: don't be caught out by unexpected blindness in front of a live audience.

Using an iPad or tablet for your notes can also solve this issue, as the screen lights up, making the room's dimmed lighting irrelevant.

27. Get them to take notes

When they are staring at a screen, your audience members are in passive learning mode. This is one of the fundamental problems with PowerPoint. When they are taking notes, however, the mode switches back to active. They must *do*, and therefore they must *think*.

There are communication consultants who will tell you that it is precisely 63.7896421 per cent more effective to have your participants do something during your speech, and that their recall efficiency will be 84.97638219751285498210 per cent greater by taking notes.

Let's get real. You can't quantify effectiveness to that degree of specificity. But we can confidently assert that getting them to do something is more effective than not doing something. And the involvement certainly does help them to remember more.

However, there is an art to speaking to an audience who are taking notes. You have to vocally separate your key learnings from the clutter; making it clear precisely what they should be writing down. If you deliver what is essentially one big block of verbiage, they won't know what to write down. As a skilful communicator, the onus is on you to emphasise (verbally and with pauses) the really important phrases.

Professional speakers tend to do this as a matter of course. The rhythm becomes second nature after a while. If you are watching a pro and taking notes, and another person at the back of the room is doing the same, and both of you are tasked with reporting back the top five points – it is highly likely that you will have recorded the same ideas, right down to identical wording.

And that doesn't happen by accident. That is a sign of professionalism on the part of a speaker who has brought the major points to the foreground using vocal emphasis and pithy wording.

He or she has learnt to separate the major sound bites from the body of the speech. Good speakers will tend to pause before and after important points, and slow down and change their tone of voice to make sure that key sentences stand out from the rest of the speech.

Let's use an example. Imagine that I am presenting about how to speak without slides. I would intentionally slow down and emphasise major points. Perhaps something like this: '... and that's the concept that great presenters understand, and that I'd like you to understand ...' (pause), 'Make sure your slides are the itch, not the scratch.'

That vocal separation – the act of highlighting the important bit – not only facilitates note-taking, but also naturally divides your ocean of words into crests and falls. It contributes to a pleasant vocal rhythm. I have sometimes heard this vocal technique referred to as 'punch, then pause'. It's a good description. Your profound idea, summed up in short, memorable wording, is the punch, and then you pause to let it sink in.

Be sure to think your way through logistics before getting your audience to take notes. If, for example, there has not been any provision for them to do so, they might feel cheated. Or you might have a rustling in the room as they search for paper. You need to have made paper and pens available.

You may find in any presentation that you do, regardless of whether you intend them to take notes or not, that some audience members will do so automatically. I see this all the time. I sometimes even make provision for it on the fly. As I say a profound line, and see that a dozen or so heads bend down to write the line out, I will pause and then repeat the line. I may even repeat it twice. Then, after allowing a brief pause, I will launch into my next segment.

The art lies in thinking in terms of how your audience is thinking, and trying to empathise with them as they process and take in your ideas.

28. Invite them to Tweet

These days, we often want our ideas to go beyond the room in which we're presenting. Sometimes, ideally, they should go viral. What better way than with a few hundred audience members channelling your grand and illustrious wisdom out into the Twitterverse? Why, you could be the next Gaga! Or worse, Bieber.

As with asking them to take notes, inviting an audience to Tweet works well if you know how to talk in catchy sound bites (of 140 characters or less).

The trick lies in how you set it up at the beginning of your speech. Tell the audience (or, if you want to look more professional, get the MC or convenor to tell the audience) that they are encouraged to use Twitter to record and publicise their thoughts. This can be positioned as a means for them to learn, while also doubling up as great exposure for you.

You should also then give them a Twitter handle or a hashtag. For instance, if I were speaking at an event for CEOs, I might give them my own Twitter handle, which is *@douglaskruger*, and then a hashtag that everyone can use to converse about the event (for instance, something like *#CEOconvention*).

A thought on Twitter walls

There is an increasing trend at conferences to announce these Twitter hashtags to the audience (which I think is great), and to then display Tweets sent to that hashtag live on the screen (which I think is horrific).

This is called a Twitter wall, or sometimes, Twitter fall. I don't like them for several reasons. Firstly, they are distracting for the audience. It's one thing to follow Tweets on your phone, but it's quite another to have them appearing on the screen behind the speaker (*#ourconference*: This guy's a dork. Anyone else notice that his fly is down?). As an audience member, I don't want to know what everyone else thinks of the presentation as they are watching it. I want to concentrate on what I think. I am not a member of the Borg Collective. I would like to think for myself.

And, secondly, from the speaker's point of view, I advocate control of the environment. And you can't control a Twitter feed. When I speak, I have the room set up according to my goals and needs, I have the lighting properly arranged, I make sure the sound system is doing what I want it to do, and I decide on the type of microphone. I've already encouraged the same for you.

I do not want an audience's passing thoughts and fancies flashing by on the screen behind me. People tend to express very freely on Twitter what they would never have the courage to say out loud, which means that the tone of the Tweets can very quickly sink to the lowest common denominator (*#ourconference*: Why did they book this fat loser? Bring back the hot chick! And when's lunch, anyway?).

I insist on total control over the time and space allotted to me. That's how I get my job done well. You should too.

And, sure, you will get compliments on the Twitter wall as well. But even these will be at the expense of your audience's concentration on what you are saying in that moment. Even the good Tweets are hype, and they detract from your content.

Where possible, I recommend insisting there be no live Twitter wall during your presentations. This is not *Idols*.

Nevertheless, asking the audience to Tweet can be a good idea. It's extra publicity and it ingrains their learning. Also, their own Tweets can act like a set of take-home notes afterwards.

29. Hand out placemats

This has to be one of the cleverest techniques I've ever seen used. And the degree to which you can customise it and make it even cleverer is staggering.

The basic principle is that you give a handout to every member of your audience. This works best in (but is by no means limited to) a boardroom context. The handout is usually about the size of a dinner placemat, which makes it big enough to be easy to see, but small enough to sit on the table before a delegate or be held on a lap. Of course, it can be any size you desire. Elephant-proportioned handouts will certainly make an impact.

The presentation structure is then laid out on the placemat, and delegates can follow your progress on their own handout.

A good, logical approach is to use a cycle around the perimeter of your placemat, like the diagram on the next page.

You can use any structure you wish, though – go for snakes and ladders if it floats your boat – but the goal is to give them a logical means to follow your flow on their own.

There is an interesting psychological advantage to using such a tool. When you are using PowerPoint, the audience cannot know how many slides remain. The slides go deep, and there is no way for them to determine how many more lie in store behind the one they are viewing, unless you do something as clunky as labelling them 'Slide 1 of 26', or announce that you have thirty-two slides to get through. Very amateurish.

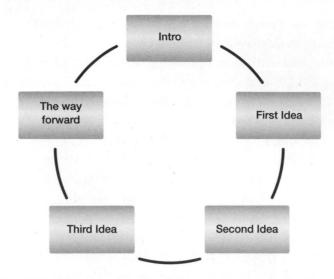

But, with this system, your audience has the certainty of knowing precisely where you are in the scheme of your total presentation at all times. They feel a degree of control, as if they have an agenda of your speech. This can help to reduce anxiety.

Getting uber-creative

You can be exceptionally creative with the placemat itself. For instance, let's say you're pitching an idea to BMW. Why not use their logo as your placemat? What a nice touch for a salesperson to hand out a guide to their presentation in the form of their prospect's logo!

Using the BMW example, you might divide your presentation into four major points, corresponding to the four quadrants that appear on their iconic badge. But, rather than simply labelling each of the four quadrants, you might overlay the badge with a second badge and a pivot through the middle, so that it functions as an independent wheel on top of the first badge. One of the four quadrants on the top badge might be cut out, revealing the information behind it (in one quadrant only). Then you and your delegates could turn the badge, like a spinning wheel, to reveal each of the four quadrants as you progress.

That's just one variation on the placemat idea. You can go to town on yours. I've just mentioned a spinning wheel. What's to stop yours from having pop-up sections, or peel-and-reveal patches, or connect the dots, or scratch 'n sniff? Of course, it doesn't even have to be in the shape of a flat placemat. Yours could be 3-D. It can be anything you want. All it has to do is give them some way to follow as you progress.

You might even turn your little placemat into a variation on Monopoly or a word search, so that your presentation leads the audience through a game, which one of them can win. Bingo!

It's novelty like this that can truly set you apart and make you memorable. From a sales perspective, the distinctiveness of such an approach can be winning, i.e. it can be worth money.

Although I don't want to place limitations on this technique, I am tempted to argue that the more complicated and interactive your placemat, the better it will be suited to small groups and boardroom presentations. It could be tricky to have 800 people in an auditorium all playing a miniature game of Monopoly on their laps. However, the example of the BMW logo would work well on pretty much any scale. You could quite feasibly have 10 000 people in the audience, all turning their little dials to keep up with your delivery.

30. Draw on a board or flip chart

Inspired, right? The kind of thing that gets parties started. Shades of Paris Hilton saying, 'That's hot!'

Actually, this humble technique can bring a unique vibrancy to your presentations. The advantage of a flip chart lies in the psychological effect of sleeves-rolled-up live creation. When we think of people writing on flip charts, we think of high-energy meetings in top-level boardrooms, as important executives work late into the night hashing out real-world stuff. We think of no-nonsense brainstorms and group input. Hence, there is a certain raw energy to a flip chart. A flip chart has a certain getting-down-to-business quality.

And it is the act of live creation that makes it compelling. There is a marked difference between revealing a large sheet of paper with a cartoon drawing on it, and actually drawing the cartoon live in front of the audience.

You've probably seen an artist drawing portraits or caricatures in a busy shopping area. Note the number of people who stop and stare. These same people might not have stopped to stare at the completed drawing. That is the power of live creation.

A bit of showmanship doesn't hurt here. If the point that you are making allows you to draw one big, sweeping line with a red marker, the effect can be profound. If you can write or draw something, and then strike it out with a massive X, you will certainly hold the audience's attention. If you can sketch out a simple cartoon, you will earn kudos.

When using flip charts, try to think of ways to create a little bit of drama. It's not just what you draw: it's the act of drawing itself. Your movement is a part of the point.

Be sure to practise beforehand, though. You might believe that you can draw a hamster riding a bicycle over a bridge, on your first attempt. But if it comes out looking like a squashed frog sitting on a cakebox on top of a rainbow, you'll be left having to explain your visual to the audience. And that's counterproductive.

Think theatre, think action, think energy. Make it live in front of them.

31. Use choreography to separate ideas

Ah, now we're really getting into the good stuff.

I first encountered this technique during a coaching session with 2004 Toastmasters World Champion of Public Speaking, Randy Harvey. Randy called it 'Speaking in 3-D'. I vividly recall feeling like a kid at Christmas when receiving the gift of this knowledge. Speaking in 3-D was like a brand-new toy and I couldn't wait to take it out and play with it. It hasn't disappointed in the years since.

So, what is speaking in 3-D? Picture yourself in the middle of an empty hall. You're facing the stage. Most people simply see an empty stage. But not you, oh no! Because you are an educated speaker – you see so much more. When you look at a stage: you see zones. You see the possibility of dividing your ideas into distinct physical spaces. You don't just see a stage: you see stories – each in its own unique setting.

Most inexperienced presenters will stand in one place (generally behind a lectern) and deliver their entire address there. Or, worse, they will pace backwards and forwards across the stage. In both cases, their use of space is meaningless. Our goal is to make the use of space meaningful. Geo-psychologically, when a speaker stands in one spot, the whole flow of information proceeds from the same place, which is dull. Or in the case of a speaker who wanders arbitrarily back and forth, the movement becomes meaningless and distracting.

But when you start to think three-dimensionally, the very space available to you on a stage can be used to visually segregate ideas. In other words, placement of sections becomes a type of visual aid.

To explain this abstract idea, let me give you a very simple example. Let's say you wanted to deliver three key points in your speech. Using choreography, you might place your first idea in the centre of the stage. You would then place the second idea, for example, on stage left and the third on stage right.

As you deliver your three key points, you subtly move to each location as you speak: point one in the middle, points two and three on the left and right. You literally walk to each location and then deliver your point from its designated zone.

With this simple technique, which most people in the audience won't even consciously notice, you will have given a visual cue that there are separate chunks to what you are saying. They will follow you more easily, even if they don't know why.

However, there are certain venues that may minimise your potential to use choreography. The example that springs readily to mind is a narrow boardroom. Although even in such a case, if you can take a step and a half to the left, and a step and a half to the right, you can place one idea on either side of you. But the concept truly comes into its own when you have a full stage available.

A brief tangent on a related topic

Inexperienced speakers often ask whether there is a rule regarding when to move and when to stand still. The answer is, no, not really. But there are some useful guidelines.

My take on the subject is this: move with intention – otherwise stand still. Moving with intention means that you might be telling a story, or getting passionately caught up in your point. By all means, move around in patterns commensurate with your passion. But when you are simply talking to the audience, stand still.

Please note that this advice refers only to your mobility in the room. Do not switch off your body language and become completely immobile. You are not a statue. Your body language should be in a natural, low-key state of action at all times. But, in terms of movement around the room, move with intention – otherwise stand still.

My personal guideline is generally this: move when telling a story; stand still when making a point. But, again, that's merely a guideline and by no means a rule.

And, now, back to our regular programming

Let's return to the idea of choreographing the stage according to segments. You are not limited to merely placing your key points in unique places. Additionally, your movement up and down and back and forth also creates certain effects, which can add vitality and nuance to your speaking.

Let's start with back and forth. If you step forward, towards the audience, the effect that you will create is a positive tone. Emotionally, such a movement says, 'Yes!' If you step backwards, away from them, the effect is negative. It says, 'No', or even, 'Beware.'

If you stand upright, the tone is simply neutral – chatty, if you like. If you crouch or sit, the tone changes entirely once again. Crouching down with your hands on your thighs creates intensity. Sitting down creates intimacy. Sitting down and leaning towards the audience creates intimacy and intensity.

Are you starting to get a sense of how far this concept can be taken? You can convey volumes with your use of space and posture. You can create distinct moods and types of energy with nothing more at your disposal than body language and spatial awareness.

Less is more?

If one idea in your presentation is profoundly more important than the rest, you can segregate it by intentionally standing in one spot for most of your speech, and then leaving the stage and walking up to the audience to deliver that one point. It will radically elevate the perceived importance of that point.

Be aware of the space in the room; be aware of how your use of up and down, and back and forth can communicate different ideas. Place your points in different locations and keep them there.

My friend and fellow speaker Jim Key, who is also a past winner of the Toastmasters World Championship of Public Speaking, often likes to deliver three major points, or three major stories in his presentations. When concluding, he gestures towards the area where he has delivered each point as he sums up the three major ideas. It works phenomenally well.

32. Use implication to create imaginary props

If you love public speaking as much as I do, take a deep breath. This is about to get cool! And if you don't, hold on tight – here we go anyway ...

You don't need to have a real physical prop in order to use a prop. You can create the impression of a prop. You can use nothing but fresh air and pretend it's a prop. And it will still work.

Does that sound eerily Zen-like and esoteric? The kind of philosophical nonsense that appears on sugar packets? *Less is more when a tree falls in the woods to the sound of one hand clapping.*

It's actually very simple. Say, for instance, you are telling a story involving a car. You would 'place' your imaginary car in a certain spot on the stage. And just by pointing to that area and indicating as if there were a car there, you will conjure up imagery in the audience's minds. You don't even need to say, 'Imagine there is a car here.' You simply gesture towards it as though it were there. Their minds will do the rest.

I sometimes use this idea, exactly as I've just described it, when I open my Expert Positioning presentation. Before even greeting the audience, I simply open with, 'It's late at night, and you're the last one to leave work. You walk out to the parking lot where there's a single car gleaming beneath a lamp. It's a BMW 7 Series – and it's yours. You take the key out of your pocket, press unlock, and it lights up like the *Starship Enterprise*. As you climb in, the door closes with that unique *whump* that seems to set the German sedans apart. Immediately, you're engulfed in an ocean of wood and leather and luxury ...' and so on.

Now here's the part that is as cool as it is curious: if you just go about it confidently enough, the audience will not even question you. They will have no problem with the use of an imaginary prop. Your conviction can utterly sell it. Just speak as if it's there, and they will watch the entire experience as though it's the most natural thing in the world.

As a sideline technical note: I greet the audience only after I've completed this first story. It adds a little theatricality.

You can see how this concept follows on from the idea of segregating your stage. We are now going one step further and placing imaginary visual aids in different locations on stage. Here's an example of how it might go, and this time I'll add in some of the cues for the speaker, so that you can imagine how the gestures and delivery might look.

'Fellow members of Luxury SUV & Sons. Last week, I walked into one of our dealerships, and there it was …'

(Point to a place on the stage.)

'Our top-of-the-line SUV. All two tons of it!'

(Indicate size.)

'The dealers had placed it beneath a spotlight.'

(Point towards the ceiling, where the audience will imagine a light shining down.)

'And the light caught its contours in the most breathtaking way!'

(Use hands to indicate light falling down and moving over contours.)

'Behind me, the manager of the dealership politely sidled up.'

(Point over your shoulder, where the audience will now picture someone, sidling up to you.)

'So, he greets me, then walks me over to his desk.'

(Walk across the stage to where you have placed an imaginary desk.)

'He shows me a chart with his sales for the month.'

(Indicate an imaginary chart on the wall.)

And so on it goes, as you paint mental pictures.

A note on delivery

Here is a subtle distinction that makes a big difference. Please note that in this example about the SUV, the cues do not indicate that you should act the part of the manager, walking up. Instead, they only say that you should point over your shoulder, to where the manager is.

You can indicate where things are and the audience will imagine them. But remember that you are still telling a story in an animated way, not acting it out.

In other words, you can say, 'I arrived at the building and walked through the door', showing where a building is and walking forward. But you must not pump your arms to indicate walking, grasp the imaginary doorknob, walk through a door and close it behind you: that will just look silly.

You are still speaking, not acting.

Indicate where items are, and your audience will see them. And if your storytelling technique is good, they will see them vividly.

Randy Harvey, in his World Championship-winning speech, described his father wearing a flannel shirt and smelling of cherry tobacco. In training courses afterwards, he would ask delegates what colour they imagined the flannel to be. The delegates all had clear answers, even though he had never provided the colour. All Randy had done was to run one hand over his arm, as though showing a flannel shirt. The audience did the rest.

Mastering this technique means that you can speak off the cuff about any topic, without a visual aid, and still 'use visual aids'. There is immense freedom in having the capacity to just 'rock up and speak'. And if you master this technique, you can do it almost anywhere, almost any time.

Take your props with you: they're all in your mind, and in the minds of your audiences.

33. Use an involvement game

In point 18, I described the game I create using a ball, a bowl and a piece of string. That was an example of an interactive prop. It was also an example of an involvement game, which is another communication option available to you in the quest to make your point. Involvement games might or might not involve props. Either way, they can be great for getting your message across.

One classic example shows the rapid spread of communicable diseases, often used to scare adolescents into practising safe sexual behaviour. It generally works like this: one person is given an identifying mark (such as a sticker or a hat), which then identifies that person as the one with the symbolic disease.

The audience members are then asked to stand up if they shook hands with that person earlier on, during the meet and greet. Once a number of people have risen to their feet, the audience is again to look at those standing and determine whether they shook hands with any of that group. If so, they are asked to stand up. By two or three rounds, most of the audience will be standing, displaying how quickly a communicable disease can spread.

Other forms of involvement games might pit one side of the room against the other; the old 'which side of the room can shout the loudest?' gambit, or the game-show style, 'Who's smarter – men or women?'

Hosted cleverly and with energy, a quiz-show type game can be fun.

34. Use the audience to demonstrate percentages

The audience itself can be a visual aid. After all, why should they just sit there comfortably while you do all the work? The lazy so-and-sos! Get 'em involved and make 'em represent something to earn their supper.

Not only does a ready-made crowd make a wonderful way to illustrate population percentages, for example, but the very act of involving them brings them into your presentation and creates heightened interest.

'Folks, could I ask the first ten rows from the left to stand up? If this audience represents the entire human population, the first ten rows represent how many people suffer from webbed toes. Truly gross! Thanks, websters, you may take your seats.'

It's much more vivid to show percentages using actual groups of people than it is to stick a pie chart up on a PowerPoint slide, or to simply say '20 per cent of people ...'

The key to using this technique successfully is confidence and assumed authority. Give the instruction like you own the place. Don't be arrogant or pushy, but give a clear, simple instruction: 'If you're in the first row, please stand.'

I find that gesturing a rising motion with my hands, and then pausing so that my body language displays that I am now awaiting their compliance, gets the request taken seriously.

Also, once they are standing and you've delivered your amazing titbit of information, give them a moment to look around the room and let a sense of the proportions sink in. Let the visual work its magic for a moment before you tell them to be seated.

35. Use audience members (or notorieties) as props on stage

People love to laugh at the boss. Can you imagine?

So, when you have the buy-in of a well-known person among the group (the rebel, the cool kid, the boss, the office supermodel), you can create a delightful vibe in the room.

I once consulted for a financial-services company with an interesting problem. The call-centre staff (who were all very young) were coming to work somewhat inappropriately dressed.

'One or two of the girls may as well be wearing handkerchiefs around their waists,' their supervisor bemoaned. 'Honestly, sometimes you can see Cuba.'

So I went and spent a week in the call centre, quietly studying the problem ... Then a few more weeks, just in case.

Of course, they could have simply pulled the old 'rant and ban' routine, but the leaders of this particular company didn't want to do that. They felt that there was already too great a degree of disconnect between the young staff and management. They were trying to build relations, not shatter them.

And so we came up with the solution of using the director of the division to make a point. A middle-aged man with a belly and a great sense of humour, he stood on a chair in front of the gathered staff as their supervisor dressed him in a series of ludicrous outfits. He went through spaceman, ballerina, rugby player and gangster rapper before we finally arrived at the short skirt and teeny, tiny top, twisted into a knot around his ample, hairy stomach.

He puffed and posed and twirled and played it up, and the laughter echoed off the windows and down the corridors. He batted his eyelids and they ate the skit for breakfast!

Then we arrived at the point. The supervisor drove it home when she said, 'Do you think he would have become the director of a division like this if he showed up for work dressed like that?'

Wiping tears away, the smiling audience replied, 'No!'

'Good, then let's discuss how you should dress to get ahead in this company. What do you think would be appropriate guidelines?'

Of course, you can do more with human props than simply stand them there. A human prop is more versatile than a mere mannequin. You can pose them, move them, or arrange them to illustrate ideas, often with great comedic effect. And the nature and physical characteristics of the person can also help to illustrate your point. On British motoring show *Top Gear*, Jeremy Clarkson once used three bikini models to illustrate the differences between three 911 Porsches.

The three bikini girls had varying … upper proportions. Sharon – he explained – was like the 911 Turbo. All natural. Vicky, however, had a bodykit … she has been enhanced and was consequently the C4S. Amanda was the Carrera 4. Enough of a handful for most men. If you'd like to watch this clip, go to:

http://www.youtube.com/watch?v=OJemsVMhEhs.

The full clip is nearly eight minutes long. If you just want to see this metaphor, skip 7:05 minutes forward.

A word of caution to using human beings as props, though: you never know what will happen, which can be meritorious or problematic. The merit lies in the spontaneous interplay of personalities, which can delight an audience. The problem is that it's all largely outside of your control.

36. Use a chair

Need a visual aid? You're sitting on one of the best!

Considering which anatomical part we park on them, chairs are one of the most venerable oratory tools in the universe. I'd go so far as to say that of all the props available to you, the humble chair is the ultimate.

Just about every venue has them and they are so versatile. They can be used for so many purposes on stage that they really are the go-to prop when there's nothing else available. If you're just a little creative, you can work wonders with a chair.

Professional speaker Robin Banks (yes, that's really his name – not his occupation) pulls a chair around the stage behind him to illustrate the drudgery of hanging on to past issues while trying to move forward in life. Every time his onstage character develops a new problem, he adds another chair, until he's pulling a stack of them across the stage. He simply lets go of the chairs when delivering his key point, which is, 'Let it go!'

In his winning speech, Toastmasters World Champion of Public Speaking Randy Harvey used a chair alternately as a car, a rock, his mother sitting on a couch and then a hospital bed. For each illustration, he would simply come back to the chair and turn it into the person or item he was talking about. It was all done so naturally that not only did you not question the use of a chair as a person, but you barely even noticed. It just worked. The chair simply was what he was talking about.

One of the most emotive uses of a chair I've ever witnessed was by Canadian speaker J.A. Gamache, who spoke at a Toastmasters World Championships contest about his uncle, who had taken ill. He gently caressed the chair as though it were the head of his dying uncle. Then, with the line, 'I'll never forget the day he passed away,' J.A. gently lowered the chair down backwards, until it was lying on its back on the stage. He did this in perfect silence and then stood looking at the chair. There was, I assure you, not a dry eye in the auditorium. The effect was magnificent.

Clint Eastwood famously used an empty chair to represent President

Barack Obama. He 'grilled' the empty chair as though it were Obama at the 2012 Republican National Convention. It's not the single greatest example of oratory you will ever see, but the concept was clever. The video is here: http://www.youtube.com/watch?v=933hKyKNPFQ

If there is no other prop or visual aid available to you, the humble chair will always be at your aid. You can stand on it for drama. You can sit on it for intimacy. You can use it as a substitute for just about anything as you tell a story. You can drag it, pick it up or get audience members to sit on it. You can hurl it, spin it, tip it over, rub it, stroke it, buy it dinner, take it home to meet your parents … you get the idea.

The simple act of standing on a chair can also serve to heighten the intensity of a segment of your delivery. I sometimes use a story illustration about performing squats at my local gym. For no reason other than to heighten the drama – I stand on a chair while explaining how squats are done. In the same way that varying your voice tone prevents you from sounding monotonous, the occasional act of rising onto a chair adds movement and visual drama to your body language.

The next time you speak, don't forget the humble chair. It's possible, just possible, that the greatest prop ever bequeathed to you as an orator is the one currently helping you to defy gravity. Your trusty chair has always held you up. It won't let you down.

37. Use your outfit

In the same way that you just might be sitting on a top-notch prop, you might also be wearing one.

A scarf, tie or handkerchief can make a magnificent prop. A shoe is not far behind (although it is traditionally considered disrespectful to lob yours at a US president, so don't). And one of the great merits of clothes as props is their capacity to hide in plain sight. You can walk to the front of the room with your hands empty, speak without hindrance, and never need a table behind which to hide and reveal your prop.

I like the visual appeal of a red tie or a red scarf, and it's amazing how much you can do with one. Sometimes when I carry out my 'throw the ball' exercise, I take off a tie and use that in place of the piece of string.

Decades back, world-renowned speaker Leo Buscaglia used to use his attire to break the ice and set the tone in an auditorium. He would arrive in a suit and explain to the audience that his mother always told him to dress to show respect. He would show the tie and say, 'I respect you! Now I'm taking it off.' The line would get a laugh from the audience, but beyond that, the act of taking off the jacket and rolling up his sleeves would communicate the idea: we're friends – now let's get down to business!

Taking off your jacket or rolling up your sleeves as you speak can be a powerful visual indicator that this particular meeting is not about hierarchy, formality or authority. By showing this cue, you indicate that the tone is about getting down to business and getting a job done. This can be very useful in settings like scenario planning or brainstorming.

38. Act it out with industrial theatre

When teaching courses on compelling writing, novelists often say that it is better to show than to tell. They explain that you shouldn't simply tell your reader that Reggie was a bitter old man, but rather present a scene in which Reggie (in a dark mood) chases a kid halfway up the block – *a-spittin' an' a-cussin'* – then kicks a dog for good measure. Now we see that Reggie is a bitter old man, having arrived at that conclusion based on what we've experienced, which is more persuasive.

Industrial theatre is the speaker's equivalent. It's the use of small skits and mini plays that illustrate your point. By way of an example, imagine that you were presenting a session on how to use body language in the workplace. Such a topic would lend itself readily to little skits. You could display a power tussle between two characters using space and intrusion of personal space on a hypothetical park bench. You could use seating arrangements in rooms, and displays of arrogance and puffery versus displays of hesitation and submissiveness, and so on.

Skits often lend themselves to 'before and after' displays – for example, 'This is Jane. She is a cowering marshmallow who gets walked all over at work. If she were part of a herd of wildebeest, she would be the sickly little one at the back, easily picked off by lions. And Jane's body language isn't helping. Observe.' Then later, 'Jane has now taken an assertiveness class and learnt how to use body language to present herself with confidence. She is no longer a sickly little wildebeest. In the previous skit, her boss just about bit her head off. Let's see if that happens again, now that Jane is armed to the teeth …'

Skits can bring a great deal of humour and vibrancy to a presentation. The acting must be rehearsed, of course, and the danger is always that it may look juvenile if not done properly. But, with a little thought, planning, rehearsal and creativity – industrial theatre can be a wonderful communication tool.

One option is to act out the various roles yourself, which can be surprisingly effective, particularly if you have any acting skills and are able to switch between characters. Use a simple prop or two, such as a wig or hat that you can easily put on or remove, to distinguish between characters.

The other option is to have your colleagues act out the various parts, allowing you to assume the role of narrator.

39. Provide handouts

Ah, handouts! Both a blessing and a curse. Some speakers swear by them, others hate their papery little intestines.

I believe that handouts are a good idea. As a delegate, I like to get home from a conference and look through all the interesting points that I learnt. It maximises the total value that I receive.

From a speaker's perspective, they're also a fabulous marketing tool because you can legitimately include all of your contact details, marketing taglines, website links and social media handles without actually looking like you're marketing to the audience. People do keep them.

But you have to be clever about your handouts. There is a bit of an art to creating them and giving them out.

For starters, let's talk timing. Do not give your handout to the audience at the beginning of your presentation. Any guesses why? 'Yes, you – the funny-looking kid at the back. Why yes, that is correct, Norman!' The answer is: because they will read the handout while completely ignoring you. Well done. Now sit back down, Norman.

Under some circumstances, it is acceptable to give your handouts to the audience mid-speech. But this depends heavily on the logistics in the room at the time. For instance, if you have one assistant and there are 2 000 people each clamouring for their sheet of paper, you cannot reasonably hand them out mid-speech. You'll end up going overtime by a couple of days.

So what is the ideal way to do it? Quite simply, hand them out at the end.

And there are a number of ways you can go about this as well. You can either have a person standing at the exit, doling out pages to people as they leave, or you can simply make them available on a desk where delegates can come and collect theirs. This creates an opportunity for them to chat with you, and for you to collect business cards. Or, and this is usually a good way to go about it, you can email your handout after the event, or make them available online using a weblink. This is often easiest done through the event organiser, but if you are building up a database, you may want to do it yourself.

Some event organisers like to have your handouts available in advance, and then include them on a flash drive, or as part of the delegates' conference packs.

Warning

Don't fall into the trap of petering out at the end by giving handouts as your conclusion. You need to end with a bang, and not a murmured, 'Okay, one for you, and one for you, and one for you ...' By ending this way, you'll rob yourself of a logical point for them to applaud.

Now, what exactly should appear on your handout? A handout can be as detailed as you want it to be. You can go for a minimalist approach, displaying only your three to five major points on a beautifully designed page. But, to be honest, a handout actually doesn't have to be pretty. Nor does it have to be small.

I remember attending an event in Dallas where I was given a handout of five pages, all stapled together, with trillions of bullet-points in teeny, tiny text, giving literally all of the information that was covered in the presentation. And I loved it! And I kept it. And I still use it.

It's worth noting, though, that you are not obliged to give handouts as comprehensive as an old *Encyclopaedia Britannica*. You can quite reasonably give a small, simple, three-point handout, which is beautifully designed and gives nothing more than a very broad overview of your topic. You get to determine what would be valuable to your audience and prepare your handouts accordingly.

Some speakers prefer not to put too much detail on the handout, believing it's like giving away their presentation. They prefer a broad overview, which would make sense to someone who attended, but not to someone who didn't. Again – your choice.

Now let's consider the marketing element of a handout. It's actually silly not to use your handout as a marketing tool. People expect it, and not to do so would be a waste of a valuable opportunity.

The simplest approach is to ensure that at least your contact details are included. But you can do more. You can include a brand logo, a photo, a visual, a tagline or a testimonial – anything you want that brings your brand to mind when people refer to your handout.

You can even go further by using your handouts to offer more. This way, instead of merely doubling up as a business card with contact details, your handout becomes an active marketing tool. For instance, you might include a line saying, 'To have Sue Sweetcheeks deliver this presentation for your team, call ...' or, 'To purchase the book on this topic, go to ...', or, 'To read free articles on this theme, visit ...' etc.

If your preference is to make your handouts more of a marketing tool than an educational one, then the design becomes important. Firstly, make sure that the printed matter looks attractive. But you can go a step further and use the shape of the handout to create novelty value.

For instance, a Douglas Kruger handout containing The Rules of Hamster Thinking could be tall and thin, like a bookmark. The top might have a hamster's head as a crest, and the material could actually be cut to the shape of the hamster head.

(Author pauses. Thinks: I should totally do that!)

People tend to keep handouts that incorporate this level of creativity. And there's nothing like a visually attractive handout displayed in someone's office to propagate your marketing message.

Put thought into the handouts that you make. Think of them first as items of audience benefit, and make them as beneficial and as valuable as possible. Then think of them in marketing terms, and make them as strong and as compelling as possible.

40. Provide incomplete handouts

Why would you provide incomplete handouts? Quite simply, so that your audience can complete them as you go!

An incomplete handout creates an air of expectation when it is received (which, in this case, has to be before your presentation), and it promotes involvement as you go along.

You *can* use this technique in conjunction with PowerPoint, but the beauty is that it renders PowerPoint unnecessary. After all, what are you planning to show the audience? The same thing that's on their handouts?

There are a number of ways that you can go about using an incomplete handout. They can either fill in text as you give keywords or phrases, or they can draw something. Or a combination of both.

If you're feeling really creative, you can even do a variation on the game Bingo. This might entail inviting your audience to look out for keywords or phrases as you go along.

The level of complexity of your incomplete handout can range from a pamphlet-sized sheet, with three or four missing keywords, right up to a full-scale manual, which your delegates use to follow along during a multiple-day boot camp.

41. Tease and reward

On its surface, this technique looks similar to the 'hint and reveal' technique explained in Part 1, but it is subtly different. When using hint and reveal, the speaker will hype up a new thing, then reveal it at the end. All along, however, we know that the new thing is, for example, the latest model of a car. We just haven't seen it yet in the flesh, so the moment of revelation is the key thing.

Tease and reward is slightly more manipulative. Slightly more cloak and dagger. The speaker does not explain a prop, but gradually allows its effect to build while the audience wonders what is going on.

Say, for instance, you have a long stage. As you speak, you lay out something that you don't explain – a line of dominoes, for instance. Then, once they are all lined up, you knock them over, to illustrate how this organisation has reached 'the tipping point'.

When understanding finally sinks in, your audience will generally laugh or applaud. Certainly, this technique always receives high praise for creativity.

And dominoes are just one possible execution. You might build something upwards, assemble the component parts of something, arrange something in a certain pattern … whatever it takes to create intrigue and, ultimately, make your point.

I once heard of a divisional manager at a bank who, in the face of a potential hostile takeover, wore a shirt in the bank's colours beneath his suit. He delivered a moving speech about the existing team and its values, then ended by opening his shirt in a Superman gesture, proclaimed, 'My blood is blue!'

The key to tease and reward is a little nonchalance and self-confidence. You need to be able to speak and carry out your activities quite casually, without succumbing to the need to explain yourself, and that requires a fair amount of discipline.

A trap to beware of: you cannot stretch this technique out over a long period of time, otherwise it will become confusing and the audience will lose interest. Your tease must lead fairly swiftly to reward. Also, this is yet another technique that requires a goodly amount of practice so that you completely master the delivery.

42. Separate and highlight

Theatre productions make use of lighting to separate and highlight important notions, moments, acts or ideas. Just think of the intensifying effect of a stage suddenly falling into darkness and a single spotlight appearing on an actor's face. It communicates the sense that it is important, therefore it has been separated from the rest – highlighted and intensified.

We don't always have the luxury of ultimate control over lighting. Indeed, it would look rather silly to drop the lights in a small boardroom and train a beam of light on your own face. It scares up imagery of kids telling one another, 'It was a dark and stormy night ...'

But there are many ways in which we can separate and highlight an important object or idea. Earlier, I mentioned that you can change your physical location and drop your voice tone in order to show that *this matters*.

You can do the same by placing an object on a pedestal, or lighting it in such a way as to make it seem important. At trade shows, important items are often lit from beneath, which can look very dramatic.

You can even separate and highlight an important phrase or quote, for example, by having it laminated on a small card and keeping it in your wallet. At the right moment, you take out your wallet, remove the card, put on your reading glasses and read the important quote. All of this puffery is really just a means of showing that the words are incredibly important, and for that reason you have separated and highlighted them.

The spirit of this technique is simply this: find a way to distinguish the important thing from the clutter, and represent it in its own space and time with an air of reverence.

43. Hand out a meaningful token

What is a meaningful token? Oddly, it is often an item that has no apparent meaning when it is first received.

A meaningful token might be anything: an apple, a card, a domino, a matchbox, a key or a coin. It could be one of the figurines from a game of Monopoly.

You hand your meaningful token to each audience member on their way in, with instructions to keep it for the presentation. Its relevance, you explain, will be revealed later. As an audience member, I am now interested in discovering the meaning and relevance of my little token and I hold onto it, intrigued.

The pay-off comes when the audience finally discovers the relevance of their item in your talk. In a best-case scenario, the meaningful token then becomes so meaningful that they want to keep it as a constant reminder of the point you made.

Imagine the success of your message if a delegate takes his or her item away, places it on the fridge at home, on a shelf, or above their computer and glances at it from time to time as a reminder of that important principle. You have effectively imbued the ordinary with a deep, almost spiritual sense of meaning.

This technique is especially well suited to presentations in which you strive to achieve buy-in – for example, when you want the audience to express greater commitment to a team, take a certain idea to heart or keep a guiding principle in mind. Your token serves to anchor this ideal.

It is generally most effective if your token in some way expresses hope. A token that focuses on a negative quality is unlikely to be kept, and might even cause resentment. You don't, for instance, want to give your sales team a reminder of how badly they missed a target, which (although I'm not suggesting it) might take the form of a tiny gargoyle pulling a tongue. Don't do that.

A meaningful token is your way of anchoring an idea in their minds and giving it longevity in their lives.

44. Burn the effigy!

Symbolic destruction: is there anything quite as satisfying?

In one of my Toastmasters contest speeches, I spoke about the idea of a grey suit – using it as an icon for a life lived in restraint and conformity. Then, at the end of the speech, I held up an actual grey suit (an old, second-hand one bought for the purpose) and set fire to it.

Burning the effigy is a very dramatic way of symbolically overcoming a negative. But, of course, your effigy needn't succumb to actual flames. It may bite the dust at the hands of water, scissors, a shredder, your tearing fingers, a raging chihuahua … or a bullet.

A Burn the Effigy presentation also requires a lot of rehearsal (and, generally, a number of trial effigies to burn).

You might be surprised at the sheer number of logistics you need to consider for this simple technique. For instance, when I burnt the suit, I had to consider:

- What to use as an accelerant: suits don't just burn.
- How to practise setting fire to a suit (without burning a number of expensive suits).
- Where to keep my matches while I spoke.
- Where to hide the symbolic suit until the moment of revelation.
- At what point on the agenda to hide it there.
- How to hold up a suit and light a match at the same time.
- Once the suit was on fire, what to do next? (In this case, I also took a drum full of water, into which I dumped the suit. It had a lid I was able to close.)
- How to get the drum full of water off the stage before the next speaker began.
- How to contain the spread of fire and ensure no safety risks were posed to the audience or venue.

In a speech I mentioned in an earlier section, I trod on a glass the way one does at Jewish weddings. Logistics for this simple act included:

- practising with exact replicas of the glass to determine how hard to stomp;
- determining where to stand on the stage so that the light caught the glass;
- figuring out how to wrap the glass in a serviette so that shards didn't render audience members blind;
- hiding the glass and serviette till the moment of revelation; and
- cleaning up shards before the next speaker on the agenda, without ending my speech on my knees with a brush and pan.

You can easily see that this technique requires a number of rehearsals to be achieved smoothly. In each case, if I had simply walked up before the audience intending to set fire to a suit or stand on a glass, I would have come crashing up against four or five unforeseen logistics hurdles.

Identifying when to use this technique is simple. The key is to ask yourself whether the core problem that your speech addresses can be represented visually by a tangible item. Then, can that item be symbolically destroyed?

I'd like to add that smoothness and subtlety are a big deal with this technique, and that overdramatisation can undo the seriousness of your point. I cringe when I recall the day, very early on in my speaking career, when I wrapped myself in chains to represent the shackles that keep us from achieving our goals, and then at the end, cast them awaaay! Melodrama is not quite the same thing as driving a point home. Be subtle, tactful and tasteful when using this technique. Done stylishly and with understated charm – and even a little humour – burning the effigy can be extremely memorable.

45. Use sleight of hand

Know a little magic? Why not use it?

Over a number of sections now, I've been banging on about the importance of concealment and revelation. If you can create your moment of revelation with a flash of smoke and a bunny, so much the better.

Naturally, this presupposes an existing skill. So, I'll keep this point short. If you have it, use it. If you don't, don't go losing sleep. There are many more alternatives.

For instance, you could always …

46. Pull an Oprah

This one takes a lot of setting up and can be expensive, but audiences love it.

At a key moment, you tell the audience to look under their chairs where – surprise! – they each find a free gift!

This works best when you want your audience to sample something or you are giving away gifts. It is therefore a logical fit with something like a sales pitch or a product demo.

Logistically, it makes sense to affix your gift to the underside of the chair using tape or an adhesive of some sort, so that your audience members don't accidentally see the free gift ahead of your big reveal.

But you're by no means limited to the underside of a chair. You could park their new S-Class Mercedes-Benz in the parking lot outside!

You can also play who's got the right key? This technique is a variation on the Oprah. Instead of giving a prize to each audience member, you give each of them a chance at the prize.

The classic example of this idea is the 'win a car' scenario, in which audience members are each given a key and the opportunity to try it out on a car. The person with the correct key wins. The people with incorrect keys spend ten minutes trying to force them into the slot anyway.

If you want to simplify your logistics, you could just do a draw: give them each a sheet of paper with numbers, then call out the winning number.

If you choose to go this route, add a little drama by reading the winning sequence of numbers one number at a time. You will find that the audience will respond with 'yes!' after each number that corresponds with theirs, and then 'no!' when their numbers stop matching – a furore that creates a great vibe.

They will also be keen to see who the winner is, so make a fuss of that person when they win. Call the winner up to the front, ask his or her name, pour confetti over his or her head, and so on.

47. Take them for a walk

In an earlier section, we discussed the use of space as a means of segregating ideas. Have you ever thought of taking this idea further than the dimensions of the room you are in? After all, the only thing confining you to the conference room is the idea that you have to stay in the conference room. There is nothing stopping you from stirring things up by taking them all for a walk.

(What? The whole audience?! Like, one great mass exodus from the room?!) Yes, precisely!

You might lead your little exodus out of the building, to a tree, for instance, which symbolises something pertinent to your topic. Whatever.

Removing your audience from the venue alters the psychology. They go from passive-receptive mode into journey mode. You take them out of their comfort zones. You intentionally introduce uncertainty, which forces them to pay attention.

The journey technique also has the effect of increasing intensity. For a great example, watch the late Robin Williams as the iconic English teacher in *Dead Poets Society*. This movie is a study in communication that works in the face of institutionalised approaches that have become dull and tired. In a way, *Dead Poets Society* represents everything I'm striving to teach and achieve with this book: be creative and get through to them.

To introduce himself to his class, the teacher played by Williams walks into the room whistling, does a tour of the desks, walks right back out again, then pops his head through the door and says, 'Well, come on!'

The boys, all slightly thrown, pack up their books and follow. He leads them to a hall where photos of previous generations of boys are displayed, spanning back decades.

Williams gathers them around, gets them to lean right in, and says:

Seize the day. Gather ye rosebuds while ye may. Why does the writer use these lines? … Because we are food for worms, lads. Because, believe it or not, each and every one of us in this room is one day going to stop breathing, turn cold, and die.

Now I would like you to step forward over here and peruse some of the faces from the past. You've walked past them many times. I don't think you've really looked at them.

They're not that different from you, are they? Same haircuts. Full of hormones, just like you. Invincible, just like you feel. The world is their oyster. They believe they're destined for great things, just like many of you. Their eyes are full of hope, just like you. Did they wait until it was too late to make from their lives even one iota of what they were capable? Because, you see, gentlemen, these boys are now fertilizing daffodils. But if you listen real close, you can hear them whisper their legacy to you. Go on, lean in. Listen, you hear it? *Carpe*. Hear it? *Carpe. Carpe. Carpe diem*. Seize the day, boys, make your lives extraordinary.

The scene ends with a severe case of goosebumps for the viewing audience … and an epiphany for the boys.

Different location, different thought patterns.

48. Get them to visually quantify their pain

I once consulted on an interesting project. A company that sold training programmes to a bank had been given a wonderful opportunity to speak at an event, before a gathering of potential customers (including financial managers, heads of departments and owners of various businesses).

Their goal, as we determined it, was to prove – and emotionalise – the fact that the real competitive advantage in this market actually boiled down to one thing and one thing only: the skill of their staff.

'As a group of industry leaders from different organisations, you are not competing against the person sitting next to you,' our speaker asserted. '*Your staff* are competing against *their staff.* And the organisation with the strongest people will win. So, how do your people stack up?'

To help the delegates visually quantify their pain, our speaker then handed out a single page to everyone in the audience. On the page was a diagram of a human form, divided into levels from top to bottom, with level one depicting the feet, level two the legs, level three the waist, and so on, like this:

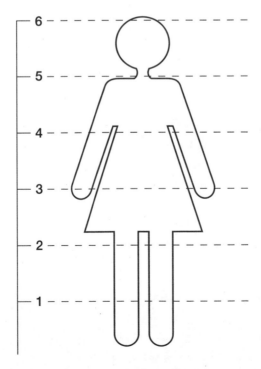

Along with their diagram, each person received three crayons. Our speaker then asked them to think of one of their typical employees – anyone who sprang to mind.

'Keep that employee in mind,' he said, 'And let's use that person as a reference point.' (Notice the use of a representative icon: one example to represent a greater whole?)

He had identified six key attributes that such an employee, in such an industry, must have, and the amount of money it might cost that company per missing attribute, if those skills were missing.

As he listed them from the stage, the delegates had to colour in a section of their diagram if their person had that quality. They used the red crayon if the person was very strong in that area, grey if they were merely competent, black if they lacked the skills entirely.

Our speaker then said, 'Take a look at your black and grey areas. Now let me tell you how much they are probably costing you.'

He then went through each of the six key attributes again, explaining the financial damage such a gap could cause in the average bank.

The genius in this illustration lay in getting delegates to visually quantify their own pain. They could see how badly they needed the solution. And putting numbers to it added immense impact too: 'If we take that person as an average in your company, your shortfall is currently costing you around fifty million per annum. If the person sitting next to you has coloured that segment in red, they are keeping that fifty million. That one thing is putting them ahead of you by fifty million. Can you live with that?'

You can quantify things in your presentations in a great many ways. Colouring something in is a good one because it takes them through a process, involving them and creating anticipation of their results, and the colours are highly visual.

But you can equally quantify pain with alternatives, such as coins. 'Get rid of a coin if the following applies to you. Gain a coin in the following instance. How many coins do you have left?'

For the sake of added impact, it's often a good idea to make the visual that you provide relevant to their world. In my example, we used an illustration of a person to represent their people. If you were addressing homeowners, you might use a visual of a house, or if you were speaking about money, you might use coins, and so forth.

The key to this technique is to take an abstract negative effect, which they might suffer, and show it to them in representative form. Make a vague idea that is difficult to grasp truly come alive by quantifying it in an undeniable way.

49. Use QR codes

What is this strange creature? QR codes are types of barcodes that your audience members can scan using their phones or iPads. For that reason, of course, this option is technology-dependent.

Once scanned by a phone, the QR code is then converted into something meaningful – the most popular options being a link to an online video clip, or your website. You often see them in magazine ads: 'Watch our video of the new BMW, tearing around a track and turning tyres into vapour! Scan here!'

You can use them to add an entirely new dimension to your handouts by incorporating video, or you can use them in conjunction with other techniques. For instance, you might pull an Oprah and combine it with the QR code. 'Under your seat is a QR code. You've won a free video clip of an S-Class Mercedes-Benz! Huzzah!'

If you're a little technologically-challenged and this concept seems utterly daunting, take heart – they are easy to create. Simply log on to www.qurify.com, and follow the prompts to create your own.

Do take note, though, that you will need to download a QR code reader for your phone before you can see it in action. QR code reader apps are usually easy to find and free to download. Also, your phone will have to have a built-in camera. If it does, and you'd like to try it out, open your scanning app and try this one:

It's a link to a YouTube clip in which I discuss how to use the stage to increase your perceived authority and total presence.

Naturally, you can use them on all manner of marketing materials as well, and professional speakers sometimes add them to products that they sell at the back of the room.

QR codes are often effective when used in a question–answer format. For instance: 'Do you know the number one secret for attracting mates of the same species? Don't get yoked to a yak. Find out what it is right here!'

It's a neat toy. Go wild with it!

50. Create a set-up in advance

This is a great technique for making a splash.

Let's say you want to elevate awareness about a topic, but it's a topic that's been covered many times and has become low-impact through simple overuse. You can revive excitement around the topic by setting up something in the room in advance of the event.

By way of example, a well-known South African media personality was speaking at a press event honouring the local police. To make a point about the police service's war against drugs, he brought a sniffer dog into the room halfway through his presentation.

The act caused quite a ruckus among the delegates. The eager dog went swiftly about the business of finding a suspicious packet, which had been planted in the room in advance for the sake of illustration.

Another dog was then brought in to find rhino horn, and did so in record time. This was obviously set up in advance (although if you happened to be in that room with an illicit stash of drugs or rhino horn ... yikes!).

The set-up was a great way to make a splash and create a buzz. But the point was just to get delegates talking about these problems. By simply speaking about them, the impact may have been fairly low. This, however (aside from the buzz it created among those present), actually made the news!

If you need to reinvigorate a tired topic, how about showing rather than telling? How about setting up a splashy display in advance?

PART 3

HOW TO USE POWERPOINT WELL ...
IF YOU MUST

'Text on a slide is not a visual aid!'
Randy Gage, International Speaker and Prosperity Expert.

Seriously? I haven't persuaded you? You *genuinely* want to go ahead with PowerPoint slides?

Fine, be that way! But let's at least ensure that when you use them, you use them well. We shall view PowerPoint as a variation on a handgun. Slides don't kill people. People who misuse slides kill people.

A compromise

What if I offered you a slight compromise? What if, instead of using an entire PowerPoint presentation, you agreed to satiate the convenors by just showing a holding slide, and nothing else? I've done it before, many times. There are even a couple of subtle advantages to it. With that in mind, we will cover the following principles for the proper use of PowerPoint:

1. Designing slides according to a hierarchy.
2. Slides should be the itch, not the scratch.
3. Using visual metaphors.
4. Rules to remember.
5. Stagecraft.

Designing slides according to a hierarchy

Here is the hierarchy of principles when designing slides, from most desirable at the top, to least desirable at the base:

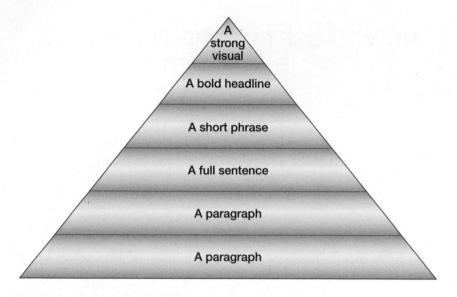

As you can see, slides with nothing but strong visuals offer a best-case scenario. Slides with multiple paragraphs written in full represent a worst-case scenario.

Differently stated: the strong presenter will show a provocative, interesting visual, and make their point using the visual as a backdrop. The weak presenter will put all their notes up on the screen and simply read them.

Naturally, you can use some items on this hierarchy in conjunction. For instance, you might design a slide showing a strong visual, along with a bold headline and a short phrase or two. That can be very effective. But the more sentences you add, the weaker the slide becomes.

Moreover, the longer the sentences you use, the weaker the slides become. It's much more effective to use a punchy phrase such as 'Rise to the top', than it is to use a full sentence like, 'A full and comprehensive examination of our recent rise to the top of the ratings table among competitors.'

Slides should be the itch, not the scratch

One of the most common problems in slide design is information dump. Speakers and presenters feel a level of anxiety before they present and to assuage their concerns, they stuff everything they know onto their slides. This way, they feel, they will be secure: 'I have the entire *Encyclopaedia Britannica* on my slides! What could possibly go wrong?'

What then happens is that they end up trying to read three hours' worth of text in their twenty-minute time slot. This creates three problems:

1. **Audience disconnect.** You sound like you're reading, and for that reason, you lose all of the magic of human connection, which is the essence and true value of public speaking.

2. **Time problems.** Everyone goes overtime – pushing the agenda (which was set to end at five) into the early hours of the next morning. Spouses file for divorce.

3. **Redundancy.** Everything's on the screen for the audience to read. So why are you even there? The speaker becomes a pointless aid to a block of text. The whole conference could have been achieved by email.

Information dumps are a bad idea. Professional communicators know that having all of the information is only half of the job. Turning it into a useful message that is suited to the audience that is present on the day is the balance.

There are a number of techniques for solving the information-dump problem. The simplest is to ensure that your slides are the itch, not the scratch. In other words, don't give the answers on the screen. Instead, pose the problem. Create the tension. Make your slides the catalyst for curiosity. This is very simply done using the upper levels of the hierarchy: strong visuals or headlines.

To further ensure that your slides are the itch, and not the scratch, use a headline that *asks* rather than one that *states*. The headline, 'Twenty per cent of people have ugly, webbed toes' is not nearly as effective as the headline, 'What percentage of people have ugly, webbed toes?' Also, the former version allows the audience to 'get it' before you say it. Once they've got it, their attention will wander off.

Asking questions is a powerful way to create audience interest and interaction. Once you've asked the question, pause for a moment and allow them to digest it. They may even suggest answers, which shows engagement. Or a perverse interest in toes. Either way, you have created a vibe in the room.

Once your slide has created the curiosity, it has done its job and it can go back to sleep. Now *you* are the show, and *you* should answer the question. The real magic is in your delivery – in your connection with your audience – not in the slide. Let the slide function as a guideline, setting up your presentation while you act as oracle, dispensing the answers.

So, the next time you prepare for an important presentation, and the temptation arises to simply dump the entire contents of your vast body of knowledge onto a slide, pause for a moment. Reconsider. Be brave. You can do better than that.

Have the courage to trust yourself. Create slides that are merely launch pads. Make your slides the catalyst for curiosity. If you put your answers on the screen, you have made yourself redundant. You might as well have just sent them an email.

The slide's only job is to set you up so that you can dive right in. No one will ever remember your slides. But if you connect with the audience, they will remember *you*.

Using visual metaphors

Ah, the return of the mighty metaphor! Earlier on, I raved about the merits of metaphors and similes. If you are going to use PowerPoint, you can darn well use them anyway!

In a presentation on economics, Kevin Lings explained the state of the national economy by showing a large ship being pulled out to sea by two smaller ships. He labelled the large ship 'government', and the two smaller ships 'lower interest rates' and 'cash liquidity', respectively.

What a superb visual for a complex subject! Talk about taking abstract concepts and helping a layperson to get it.

I occasionally use a striking visual for my keynote speech on Hamster Thinking. It's a scene on a soccer pitch, in which all of the players have boxes over their heads. I have yet to find a better visual representation of corporate hamster thinking, in which bosses tell their staff what to do, but not why, effectively hamstringing them from using their initiative.

I tell audiences that hamster thinking works like this: the boss will tell his staff member to run three steps forward and kick. Technically, that should work. The ball is three paces away. But if anything changes, the instruction will become meaningless. And the staff member cannot adapt because he doesn't know why he's running three steps forward and kicking. To build initiative, we need to teach our staff that they are playing soccer, and not instruct them to take three steps forward and kick. If they understand the bigger picture, they can react and adapt.

Rules to remember
- Keep the number of slides to a minimum. Your slides should be the itch, not the scratch.
- Whenever possible, use visuals rather than text.
- Keep special effects to a minimum. Yes, you can create a slide that whirls in out of the mists of oblivion, twirls around three times, changes colour and pulsates with flashing lights. But it will undermine the level of your presentation. If you do use lines of text, they should ideally just appear on the screen, or at most, fade in, fly in, or dissolve. Nothing fancier than that. If you are going to have items fly into the screen, make sure that they all fly in from the same side, at the same speed, without sound effects. Less is more.
- If you must use text, choose keywords over paragraphs. When you use paragraphs, people will read your slides rather than listen to you.
- Questions are often more intriguing than statements. Your slide can ask a question, which you then answer.
- When using strong visuals, bring the slide up and allow a moment of silence for the audience to take it in. Then start speaking.
- Conclude what you are saying about a particular slide before you bring up the next one, otherwise your vocal rhythms will start to show that the slides are pushing you along, and not the other way around. Have the confidence to pause while changing slides.

Stagecraft

That covers the basics of slide design. Now let's step outside of the design mindset and think about how you, as the speaker, can best interact with slides. Here are some guidelines for delivering your presentations:

- Practise using your PowerPoint in the context of your speech before you even think about using it in front of a live audience. Go through it, practising aloud: 'I will say this, and ... (click) ... Then I will say this, and then ... (click) ...'
- Check that you will have an opportunity to set up between presentations. One of two things is likely to happen: either you will have to unplug someone else's laptop and plug yours into the projector, or you will be asked whether you have your presentation saved on a flashdrive so that it can be used on the computer that is already plugged in. It's wise to prepare for both cases. It's also a good idea to have someone else set up your computer when possible, so that you don't have to struggle with equipment while you should be thinking about content.
- Never stand between your audience and the slides. Ideally, you should arrange the screen off to the side so that you can stand front and centre, and command the space. If that isn't possible, stand off to the side, so that you are not in the light, or use a remote clicker to blank the screen so that you can walk through the projector's beam area. If you don't have a remote clicker, press B or W on your laptop to blank the screen – see below.
- Never talk to your slides: talk to the audience.

A couple of cool tricks on PowerPoint

In presentation mode:

- Press B to turn the screen black (and B again to return it).
- Press W to turn the screen white (and W again to return it).
- Press Control + P to turn the mouse into a writing pen.
- Press E to erase what you've written with the pen.
- Press Control + H to remove the pen.

There. I feel dirty. But it's done!

FINAL STORY: YOUR MISSION, SHOULD YOU CHOOSE TO ACCEPT IT

Here's your challenge: there are 120 rural women in a small town in South Africa. All are over the age of forty, and they're packed into a community hall in the middle of nowhere. They're hot, they're sweaty and they've gathered to hear another speaker. Not you – but your bank – is sponsoring the event. Get them excited about opening an account with you. Go!

Actually, it is possible. But you'd really have to zero in on their interests and speak to them on a human level. You'd have to capture their imagination and show them, in practical ways, how they will get something from what you're offering.

Sadly, that's not what happened when I actually watched a presentation with precisely those parameters.

The besuited speaker – glaringly segregated from the group by his outfit alone – spoke passionately about 'onboarding' them. He described, in minute detail, the administrative process they would go through during the 'customer-uptake' stage.

They stared uncomprehendingly. So did I.

Did I mention that English was not their first language? To be fair, it wouldn't have helped if it had been. Onboarding is not even in the English dictionary. It's pure, unadulterated marketese: jargon of the most self-indulgent kind.

I've rarely seen a marketing effort fail with quite such spectacular aplomb! He may as well have spoken Russian, described the workings of a nuclear power station – and yodelled it all for good measure – with the hall lights off.

So, what went wrong? Quite simply this: the actor took his script on stage. Instead of acting the part, he read his cues aloud. He spoke *marketing* to them, instead of *human being*.

Are you reading out your script?

True marketing gurus understand that their in-house jargon is incredibly useful. To *them*. And of precious little interest to their target market.

By all means, when tucked away behind boardroom doors, flood your strategy sessions with 'onboarding', 'upselling', 'monetising' and more. But to use that terminology when speaking to your customers is to simply confuse them. Or worse, to reveal that you are aiming a technique at them. Those words are your script. They are your cues. They are not to be read aloud before the audience.

Think of it in terms of a Shakespearean play. The best plays don't look like plays. They are so real, so vivid and so incredibly authentic that you forget you're actually watching a paid professional go through practised motions. You become entranced by the story.

Speaking marketese to your clients is like walking on stage and pro-claiming, 'I am the character Romeo! Now watch as I walk to stage left, where I shall deliver yonder emotional speech to fair Juliet, the role of whom will be played tonight by Janet Bloggs, from Smalltown, Middle-burg. This is gonna totally make you cry, I promise!'

Practised marketers know that their job is to make magic, appeal to people and ultimately sell their products and services. The more real – the more authentic your message – the less people feel they are being 'techniqued' at. Great art is the art of hiding the art.

Your Copernican Revolution for the day

There is a backstage and an onstage to what we do. When you're back-stage, you need to speak like a marketer, think like a marketer – use all that wonderful marketing jargon that tipples off your tongue so satisfy-ingly. But when you get on stage, you must speak a different language. You cannot use marketese before your audience. You will ruin the play.

When the moment arrives, when you take the stage and they're all watching – that's when the magic must happen.

Here's how I would have gone about this presentation had I been the man from the bank. I would have opened with a series of questions, pitched at the level of the audience, to create a connection and engage their interest: 'Do you sometimes worry about how prices keep going up while salaries stay the same? Are you finding it harder to buy groceries every month? What are you planning to do if bread gets any more expensive than it already is?'

Then I would have progressed on to a simple explanation of how my bank might help them. 'There are five things that we can do for you.' For each bullet point, I would have told a simple, mini story, depicting how the audience members would be better off as a result of the bank's services.

Then I would have ended with a call to action. 'Please enjoy the presentations that we've arranged for you today, and before you leave, come and see me at the back. I'll help you to sign up, and we'll start making your life better from tomorrow.'

His entire presentation could have taken five minutes, and it would have been exponentially more effective than the self-serving mumbo-jumbo he subjected them to.

So, search your heart. Search your vocabulary. Seek out and excise all those precious pearls that make you feel like an important marketing mogul. Now remove them from your speeches, your ads, your scripts, your Tweets and your blogs. Your job is not to flatter yourself with displays of linguistic self-love and incestuous references to your own world. Your job is to make ideas come alive and sell.

To do that, you must appeal to their minds, their hearts, their imaginations. You must speak powerful *human being*. You must tell audience-centred stories. If you do, they will buy from you. They will buy into you. And that is a sign of a true expert.

Hide the script. Ditch the slides. Speak *human*.

Be interesting. And happy persuading!

REFERENCES

Anthony, Ray, and Barbara Boyd. *Innovative Presentations for Dummies.*
New Jersey: John Wiley & Sons, 2014

Buzan, Tony, and Barry Buzan. *The Mind Map Book.* London: BBC Active, 2006

Kahneman, Daniel. *Thinking, Fast and Slow.* New York: Farrar, Straus and
Giroux, 2011

Tufte, Edward. *The Cognitive Style of PowerPoint.* Connecticut: Graphics
Press, 2003

About the author

Douglas Kruger is the only person to have won the Southern African Championships for Public Speaking a record five times. As a result of winning this contest, hosted annually by Toastmasters International, he has regularly represented Africa at the World Championships of Public Speaking. In 2004, at the age of twenty-three, he placed second in the world – the highest ranking anyone from Africa has ever attained. In 2014, he was invited to be a guest speaker at the Toastmasters Global Convention in Kuala Lumpur, where he spoke on the topic Own Your Industry – How to Position Yourself as an Expert, based on his book with Penguin Random House South Africa. Douglas is also the author of *Relentlessly Relevant – 50 Ways to Innovate*, published by Penguin Random House South Africa in 2015.

He is a full-time professional speaker and business author. Based in Johannesburg, he speaks and trains all over the world, helping corporate clients to position themselves as industry experts and sharing the underlying principles of talent. He also helps brands innovate in order to remain relentlessly relevant.

Douglas has spoken for audiences of every imaginable shape, form, type and description, from three people in a broom closet (true story!) to 3 000 professionals in an auditorium. He has spoken in prisons and at schools, in boardrooms and on TV, at churches and for global conferences. And he knows precisely what goes wrong in speeches and presentations, and how to avoid these errors.

He has coached high-level executives and CEOs of brands like BMW SA, Samsung, Microsoft, Liberty, FNB and more. Douglas is a passionate advocate of avoiding PowerPoint in presentations or, at a minimum, learning how to use it well.

In addition to his books, he is also the producer of several motivational video and audio programmes.

Douglas sincerely and humbly hopes that *How to Make Your Point Without PowerPoint* will earn him a Nobel Peace Prize for services rendered to humanity (based upon the global suffering he hopes to alleviate by freeing desperate corporate audiences from the human-rights violation of terrible slides – a global scourge and the single source of modern humanity's greatest misery).

See him live in action, read his inspirational articles, or sign up for his free motivational newsletter at www.douglaskruger.co.za. Follow him on LinkedIn, or on Twitter, using @douglaskruger.